A Technical Excellence Framework for Innovative Digital Transformation Leadership

Transform enterprise with technical excellence, innovation, simplicity, agility, fusion, and collaboration

Dr Mehmet Yildiz

Distinguished Enterprise Architect

First Edition, August 2019

Copyright © Dr Mehmet Yildiz

Publisher: S.T.E.P.S. Publishing Australia

P.O Box 2097, Roxburgh Park, Victoria, 3064 Australia

info@stepsconsulting.com.au

Edited by Mark Longfield

Disclaimer

Table of Contents

Chapter 1: Introduction

Purpose of this book

The primary purpose of this book is to provide valuable insights for digital transformational leadership empowered by technical excellence by using a pragmatic five-pillar framework. This empowering framework aims to help the reader understand the common characteristics of technical and technology leaders in a structured way.

Even though there are different types of leaders in broad-spectrum engaging in digital transformations, in this book, we only concentrate on excellent technical and technology leaders having digital transformation goals to deal with technological disruptions and robust capabilities to create new revenue streams. No matter whether these leaders may hold formal executive titles or just domain specialist titles, they demonstrate vital characteristics of excellent technical leadership capabilities enabling them to lead complex and complicated digital transformation initiatives.

The primary reason we need to understand technical excellence and required capabilities for digital transformational leadership in a structured context is to model their attributes and transfer the well-known characteristics to the aspiring leaders and the next generations. We can transfer our understanding of these capabilities at an individual level and apply them to our day to day activities. We can even turn them into useful habits to excel in our professional goals. Alternatively, we can pass this information to other people that we are responsible for, such as our teenagers aiming for digital leadership roles, tertiary students, mentees, and colleagues.

We attempt to define the roles of strategic technical and

technology leaders using a specific framework, based on innovation, simplicity, agility, collaboration, fusion and technical excellence. This framework offers a common understanding of the critical factors of the leader. The structured analysis presented in this book can be valuable to understand the contribution of technical leaders clearly.

Admittedly, this book has a bias towards the positive attributes of excellent leaders on purpose. The compelling reason for this bias is to focus on the positive aspects and describe these attributes concisely in an adequate amount to grasp the topic so that these positive attributes can be reused and modelled by the aspiring leaders. As the other side of the coin is also essential for different insights, I plan to deal with the detrimental aspects of useless leaders in a separate book, perhaps under the lessons learned context considering different use cases for a different audience type. Consequently, I excluded the negative aspects of useless leaders in this book.

Audience

This book can be an ideal source for those who strive to become excellent technical or technology leaders aiming to lead proliferating digital transformation initiatives in these fascinating times of technology leadership. This book can guide anyone interested in understanding the characteristics and essential capabilities of excellent technical and technology leaders engaging in digital transformation programs.

This book can be of particular interest to those who hire talented technical leaders for transforming organisations. These recruiters can create a checklist of the identified characteristics and capabilities to fit into the senior digital leadership roles they try to fill in.

This book can also be useful for students studying technology leadership and want to understand the practical aspect of technical leaders and technology leadership in the digital market. As leadership is a transferable skill, this book can be of interest to anyone who wants to sharpen their digital leadership skills by reviewing the framework details.

Observations from my background

In my information technology career, over the last three decades, I worked with hundreds of technical leaders in various companies and client organisations. My engagements with these leaders helped me accumulate valuable knowledge and insights into the recognisable attributes and characteristics of these esteemed technical leaders. These technical leaders can be roles models for many of us striving for excellence. I modelled some of them for my technical leadership positions.

Some technical leaders left terrific impressions on me. I still remember those I met over 30 years ago. They were special. Something was overtly different in their leadership. These leaders touched me at a personal level from multiple aspects. Some made me feel confident to participate in their engagements hence obtained my support quickly. Some were nurturing and helped me achieve my goals effectively. Some made me think in strategic directions and got benefits of my thinking skills while they were teaching me new strategic skills. These mutual interactions established win-win situations for leaders and followers.

As opposed to excellent leaders, some incompetent leaders left undesirable impressions on me. They had the authority to lead; however, they did not have the credibility and capability to demonstrate. Their approach was depicting obvious self-interest. They were hiding behind their titles and mandating people to work for them for their self-interest to promote themselves rather than empowering others or exceeding company goals. Those type of leaders did not survive long as they did not get the full support of their followers. After a while, they had no followers. With no support and further choices, they sadly left their organisations; perhaps their career too. In this book, I don't dwell on this type of useless leaders. They are out of scope.

We are always impressed by influential technical leaders. They inspire and motivate us to reinvent ourselves. Influential leaders are principle oriented and the type of leaders, talking the talk and walking the walk with integrity. We sense their fabulous presence when they approach a venue to connect with us. They are so attractive and welcoming that we comfortably seek their advice and guidance.

Having these insights based on my interactions with technology leaders coming from different walks of life, I created a collection of their skill sets and demeanours in a digital repository. Some of these leaders served me as my mentors, and I closely interacted them at a personal level. Some were my first-line managers, and we had a manager-employee relationship in addition to their technical leadership services. Some were my second line manager or executives, and I only talked with them when they needed me.

However, even though our encounters happened less frequently, there was still some close relationship in our communications. Some were my peers, and we had excellent peer relationship and intimately talk about anything from personal to professional matters. Some were my lecturers and supervisors, during my studies, who broadened my horizons. Whatever formal role they had, we had some constant professional interactions leading to mutual learning and development. I want to share this learning with my readers.

Even though they all were people and process-oriented for their roles, one key observation was that all technical leaders I worked with were passionate about technology at personal levels. They embraced technology matters and ingrained them to their behaviour. They reflected the technological passion in their communications and day to interactions. This common factor -a passion for technology- is worth mentioning to recognise technical leaders.

Since I mainly worked with the technical and technology leaders, I documented their characteristics based on my fieldwork spanning over 30 years. These documents included voluminous diary notebooks, which I digitised in the last ten years using character recognition and conversion technologies. As part of my doctoral and post-doctoral studies, I also researched broad technical leadership, cognitive capabilities, and learning patterns of technical leaders. As part of my studies and personal interest, I performed a comprehensive literature search on the field to validate my hypotheses and findings. Therefore, these three primary input sources triangulated my views to create the framework I present in this book.

To make the book easy to read and not to bore the busy readers, I followed a practical approach to the matter and refrained from the scientific claims, long theoretical discussion, and citations hence provided a conversational style narration to transfer my compelling message effectively and concisely based on my knowledge and practical experience in the field.

Summary of Methodology

You can skip this section if you are convinced with the prior section on my approach. However, I think it is necessary to provide a brief background on the approach I used to research, analyse and collide this book.

One of the best habits I gained in my undergraduate

studies in the early 80s was keeping a personal, a study and a work journal. One of our wise lecturers thought us that nothing recorded nothing happened in life. He mentioned that our journal entries in later parts of our lives would shed lights on our identity, and they would be invaluable sources of information to know about ourselves. With these compelling reasons, I made it a habit to keep journals during my studies and sustained the habit over the last 30 years in my professional life.

I created a few diaries in hard copy on those days one about personal life, one about my professional learning on technical matters and the most interesting one for this book was the leadership observations and learnings. These journals stemmed from my day to day interactions with leaders from the field and included my leadership journey starting with a team leader of a technical development team then flourishing to multiple more advanced technical leadership roles after many years.

As part of my doctoral studies, I digitised hard copies of my diaries to a single digital format which turned to a searchable and editable version for text analytics. Since then, I only have a single digital copy of my journal, which is fed by my mobile phone entries, blogs, work journals and multiple other agile collaboration tools. In recent years, I managed to incorporate to my journal other formats such as picture, sound and videos as well.

While analysing the content for writing this book, I extensively utilised these journal entries consist of my recorded observations developed over the years. I performed unstructured data analysis techniques to identify the relevant points to triangulate my ideas, observations, and findings in the literature. These unstructured pieces of text consist of my observations and interactions provided a rich source of data sets to support my views and findings.

I applied some pattern recognition techniques such as using keywords and phrases, then followed up relevant entries and explored them further for details by analysing them to support the core concepts in this book.

My journal included many sentiments recorded related to the situations in the workplaces. These sentiments included interactions with hundreds of technical and technology leaders responsible for different aspects of information technology. Most recently, in the last 10 years, I am a hands-on technical transformation leader for many large organisations. I still keep a journal of my daily interactions and critical learning points even in further detail thanks to various mobile devices which made journal entries much easier compared to 80s.

After analysing my 30 years of unstructured data in journal entries, I stripped off the bad experiences and negative attributes and filtered all the positive experiences as the selected content for this book. The purpose of this methodological reason was to provide my readers with crucial aspects of excellent technical and technology leadership, which can be reused and modelled. Of course, the bad attributes and negative experiences matter and I value them as lessons learned; however, I aim to analyse them for a different book planning for different use cases for my potential readers. Enough about the methodology and let's start learning about the fundamentals of technical excellence.

Chapter 2: Fundamentals of Technical Excellence

Defining Technical & Technology Leaders

Even though these terms are used interchangeably in literature and the workplace, there are subtle differences amongst them; hence, I see a necessity to define and point out the key differences here.

The main difference between a technical leader and a technology leader is the nature of the roles and responsibilities they hold in an organisation. Technical leaders can lead technology initiatives using their extensive technical expertise; however, they may not have a management role and not accountable for human resource activities such as assessing people's skills, organising their payroll, promoting or ending their employment.

Technical leaders may have titles such as Chief Engineer, Lead Software Engineer, or Lead Enterprise Architect. On the other hand, technology leaders usually have traditional roles in managing a team or department responsible for technology initiatives. Technology leaders have commonly known titles of CTO (Chief Technology Officer), CDO (Chief Digital Officer), CIO (Chief Information Officer) or Head of Technology. These titles may vary in different organisations and geographies.

However, these roles, especially in smaller organisations or startup companies, can be combined under a collective name such as the head of technology. In some small organisations, these roles might have no position of power, such as managing no people but purely responsible for the departmental function. For example, a CTO in a startup company is accountable for all technical matters, making decisions, and doing follow-ups with no departmental management responsibility and having no direct reports as opposed to the CTOs working in large organisations with many direct reports under them.

Another observation for the difference between technical and technology leaders is that technical leaders cover more of depth rather than breadth in general. For example, a chief software engineer mainly focuses on software technology, processes and tools and may have an only broad perspective on other domains such as infrastructure, hardware or data.

Whereas, a CTO has a broader scope for understanding all technologies, processes and tools deployed in an organisation without going too much into detail in each domain as these CTOs are responsible and accountable for making informative decisions for business executives. Rather than assessing and analysing each situation, a CTO may delegate those details to relevant specialists and integrate the findings in a coherent story for the business stakeholders. Telling a compelling story for technical matters is a challenging and critical skill itself hence makes the role of CTOs quite demanding and unique in transforming organisations.

However, some particular technical leaders or technology leaders can cover both the breadth and the depth in their roles. These so-called T-shaped leaders are scarce resources, exceptional, and continuously in demand to lead integrated domains with high impact transformational missions. Some of these distinguished technology leaders while holding a breadth of technical knowledge in all domains, they also are capable of having specialist level knowledge in multiple subdomains. More fascinatingly, it is even possible to encounter some practical leaders who have hands-on experience in some technology domains at a specialist level. However, these hands-on technical or technology leaders are in the minority rather than the majority.

Realistically, for a conventional technology leadership role in large organisations, the breadth of knowledge for technology, processes, and tools is more critical than having a depth of knowledge in a single area. Covering breadth can help the technology leaders to see the big picture and articulate complicated situations to business stakeholders effectively without clouding the topic with unnecessary details. However, these technical and technology leaders need to be capable of gauging the veracity of the delegated analysis to provide a coherent view.

Exceptionally, I met some CTOs who understand the technologies at a broad spectrum, but they are also very knowledgeable, at a specialist level, in certain technology domains such as cybersecurity, distributed networking, application development processes, directory services, and many other domains. These professionals usually worked as technical specialists in multiple domains and initiatives, then promoted to a CTO role towards the end of their employment in an organisation, usually after several decades of long service. We usually refer to them as 'silver-headed leaders'.

Another common characteristic of technical and technology leaders is that both types of leaders get involved in both tactical and strategic matters as far as broad sets of technologies are concerned. While they participate in day to day running of the technology departments or specific domains at a tactical and operational level, they also look at the strategic aspects by developing long term technology roadmaps for their planned and progressing technology goals, especially for digital transformations.

Considering differences and similarities, even though there are subtle differences between technical and technology leaders, there are significant overlaps in their roles and responsibilities. Therefore, rather than separating them as technical or technology leaders, I propose to call them 'excellent digital transformation leaders' because both types of leaders focus on transforming their environments to more agile, simplified, innovative, collaborated, and excellent service organisations.

Working with hundreds of these excellent digital transformation leaders, I came across five distinct primary enablers for excellent leadership to survive and thrive in digitally transforming organisations. I'd refer to these enablers as five pillars for excellent technical and technology leaders. These five pillars are innovation, simplicity, agility, technical excellence, and productive collaboration with fusion. We cover each pillar in subsequent chapters and sections.

Excellence versus perfection

Excellence may mean different things to different people. My definition of excellence for the scope of this book is specific and applies to the recognisable attributes of technical leaders. Excellence in this book refers to having or demonstrating outstanding quality for the leaders for making a noticeable impact on other people, especially on the followers of these leaders. The outstanding quality comprises the leader's knowledge, skills, experience, expertise, and personality traits.

There may be a potential misconception that excellence means perfection. It does not. We need to clarify that excellence and perfection are not the same things. Perfection ironically can be a deterrent to excellence. Those who aim for perfection, as a side effect, can face procrastination and unnecessary effort to achieve so-called perfection, which is usually not realistic. Perfection is difficult to attain, almost impossible human endeavour. The cost of perfection is prohibitive and undesirable. There is even a term coined in the corporate world called "gold-plating". This term refers to perfection efforts, which results in no financial gains.

Even though some may pursue of perfection in their endeavours, it is not possible to reach consensus for an understanding of perfection. Since we are individuals and all have different filters in our minds, we see perfection differently. For example, an outcome which may be classified as perfect for one person may not necessarily be considered as perfect by another. Different value judgements may have different implications for recognition of perfection.

Therefore, excellent leaders never strive for perfection; instead, they focus on excellence. As a simple example, one may provide an excellent effort using 90% of our energy for a well-accepted solution, however, using an extra 9% to reach a 99% close to perfection level can be too costly. We all know that realistically no solution can get a 100% consensus when judged by a large group of consumers even though it may exceed its goals from multiple angles.

After highlighting the importance of pragmatic excellence, rather than pie in the sky type of perfection, let's now move on and touch on the other compelling attributes that genuinely matter for excellent leaders and make a significant impact on their success especially for transformational goals.

Tolerance to uncertainty or ambiguity

Tolerance to uncertainty and ambiguity is a well understood and accepted leadership attribute. Leaders deal with future outcomes. They make the future. However, the future is unknown to us as humans, as outcomes are affected by a myriad of causes beyond the control of people. Therefore, uncertainty is a reality to deal with future events.

Uncertainty is a closely related term to risk management. Taking risk is one of the necessities and most fundamental characteristics of leaders for success. Risk and opportunity are like inseparable yin and yang. We can even simplify at the most basic level that no risk, no opportunity. Leaders know that opportunities are created by taking risks. They take calculated risks using their logic and intuition and mitigate them to be able to deal with uncertainty in a systematic way. One of the techniques they use is to learn from past failures and use these learnings in their risk-taking engagements.

Dealing with uncertainties and ambiguities creates new options and choices leading to innovation. Having more options to choose and linking those options in a creative, an intelligent, and the integrated way can create new transformational solutions. To this end, digital transformation that excellent leaders strive to require tolerance to uncertainty and ambiguity by taking calculated risks to create opportunities leading to desired digital transformations.

Emotional Intelligence

Dealing with people and leading teams require robust emotional intelligence. Emotional intelligence (EQ) requires awareness and management of one's own emotions and understanding others' emotions too. Those leaders with high EQ can handle interpersonal relationships more effectively and empathetically.

Empathy and compassion for others have a magical impact on the leaders and their followers. This natural human need is genuine and experienced in all social settings. We can communicate better by using empathy for the others whether they are our peers, superiors or subordinates. Consideration of other's unique circumstances with empathy can open the communication channels for leaders.

Emotional intelligence also makes the leaders more self-aware with their fluctuating moods, changing emotions, and drives. This self-awareness makes a tremendous difference when dealing with people. Once they are aware of their moods and emotions, they can take appropriate actions for their communication and interactions with others. Self-awareness also helps with self-regulation. They can make better decisions by delaying their gratifying urges for immediate responses, which may not necessarily serve to their best interest at the times when they are experiencing low moods and debilitating negative emotions.

Emotionally intelligent leaders behave authentically. Their behaviour reflects their authentic self in their communication and interactions with others. They align with their principles based on authenticity. This authentic behaviour is noticeable and welcomed by others. Authentic leaders do not fear to show their vulnerabilities. Paradoxically, showing their human vulnerabilities to others, empowers them, make them more confident, more balanced, and even makes them stronger leaders. I observed these type of leaders in my engagements and their vulnerability made them more credible in my eyes.

Even though a certain amount of IQ is necessary for technical foundations and overall organisational structures, EQ makes the difference for leadership excellence. Technical leaders deal with people day to day, their success is dependent on other people, and these leaders motivate their followers not only for being productive for work purposes but also for finding the best version of themselves.

Being Mindful

Mindfulness is a widely researched and well-understood topic for all kinds of leaders. Mindfulness applies to technical leaders, too, and they can benefit from mindful approaches. Arguably technical leaders may need mindfulness more than any other type of leaders due to the additional stresses they have in their lives and rapidly changing complex work environments. Mindfulness enables technical leaders to become emotionally intelligent. Emotionally intelligent and mindful leaders demonstrate empathy, compassion, and acceptance. Mindful leaders behave confidently and develop healthy work relationships.

Mindful leaders can cope with massive stress caused by hectic workplaces, volatile business situations, and ever-changing technologies effectively. Their unflappable attitudes can be inspirational and make them role models in coping with stress in their teams. Mindful leaders also develop strong intuitions due to clarity they generate in their minds.

As mindfulness improves one's attention, the mindful leaders can also be more productive and creative by focusing on the things that matter for their goals and plans. By using mindfulness, these leaders eliminate distractions and sharpen their mental power for essential matters to achieve their aspirations and transformational goals for their organisations.

To exemplify the importance of mindfulness for technical leaders, I'd like to share one of my observations in a paradoxical situation in critical circumstances at work. When a disaster happened in IT operations area affecting thousands of users due to a system or an application failure, one leader was calm and composed, but another leader was agitated and disturbed. This difference was apparent to the whole team, and people were wondering the difference between two types of leaders responding differently to the same situation. The impact of mindfulness of the technical leaders was an observable experience in the workplace.

Mindfulness also helps technical leaders to keep things

in the right perspective and context. Attention and focus on the right perspective provide clarity for seeing the right context. This positive behaviour also aligns people, brings them on the same page, unites them for mutual goals, and directs their attention on the right context. Staying connected in the right context and medium is a prime position to be in for transformations to happen.

Being mindful and acting with emotional intelligence make the leaders calm, composed, and unflappable during critical situations. With these magical benefits of mindfulness for technical leaders, they can communicate better, act better, obtain better support, and produce better outcomes collectively.

Personal Responsibility

Taking personal responsibility in all walks of life is a virtue for all humans. This foundational human attribute is a particular empowering capability for the technical leaders. Taking personal responsibility and being accountable for the situations we create, we can leave better impressions on other people. This positive disposition creates a trust for our integrity.

As opposed to taking responsibility, complaining about situations and blaming others and circumstances for undesirable outcomes create a negative atmosphere in workplaces. Blame removes the power and replaces it with weakness. Blame, whatever the circumstances are, creates an undesirable situation in the workplace as no one enjoys taking the blame even if they are on the wrong side of the fence.

Excellent leaders are aware of the implications of blaming and complaining; hence, they always take personal responsibility for their actions, emotions and results they produce. These leaders also encourage everyone in their teams to do so. When everyone in these teams takes personal responsibility for their actions, the culture shifts to a pleasant situation. People become more responsive and transparent. A culture of trust is built. People act with integrity. Because of these empowering benefits of taking personal responsibility at work, technical leaders can perform better and produce outstanding results for their digital transformational goals with these culturally transformed people.

Action Orientation

Knowledge and skills without action do not produce any desired outcome in the workplace. Excellent leaders are aware of this well-known fact; consequently, they are action-oriented. Excellent leaders prioritise their tasks and act immediately based on their priorities. They don't like delaying necessary actions. They dislike procrastination unless something in their list is shallow value, low priority, have other dependencies, and have an extended time to complete.

Actions are taken using practical tools and processes in the workplace. Using a quick phone call rather than writing a long email can be more effective in taking action for a priority matter. Sometimes making multiple phone calls with different stakeholders, bringing them in the same room with a clear agenda for a short time can help resolution of complicated matters much more effectively. These practical action-oriented techniques are well known and used by these leaders.

Sometimes taking action for complicated matters can be a daunting task for the team members. These technical leaders can help the team members to deconstruct the enormous tasks to smaller components and deal with each piece in priority order. Besides, excellent leaders check the progress actively, encourage people to keep going with their actions, and they do regular follow-ups to ensure they succeed at all times. Excellent leaders are not only action-oriented by themselves, but they also enable others to become action-oriented by facilitating the activities, making the approach easier, clearing the hurdles, and providing a clear vision.

Vision

Vision is a metaphorical term referring to our mental picture of the future. We develop our ideas for future events and outcomes which establish our vision. Leadership in any area requires having a vision. More importantly, articulating the vision and influencing the followers are the essential traits of technical leaders.

It is the vision which attracts the people towards their leaders. Team members need to have confidence in their leaders' vision to reach common goals. Leaders' vision inspires the followers to work for them more efficiently and support them wholeheartedly. It is the meaning added by the magic of vision set by the leaders. The term visionary leader highlights the importance of vision for leaders. Excellent technical leaders are known for their visionary skills.

Leadership vision needs to display the values, beliefs, and culture of the organisation. Leaders' vision brings team members together; hence, they work for the same goals. Without a well-communicated and clearly understood vision, people get lost in complicated organisations process and procedures. Vision sharpens the team members focus and empowers them to work in the same direction.

Social Intelligence

Social intelligence, related to emotional intelligence, knowing about one's self and the dynamics of other people around us. Interacting with people and feeling comfortable with many personalities is a core requirement of social intelligence. Excellent leaders are socially intelligent people. They participate in social situations and enable other people to engage with others socially in the workplace.

Some necessary social skills for excellent leaders are listening to others authentically, being emphatic, responding genuinely, sharing thoughts openly, and influencing them to realise their goals. Excellent leaders bring people together for an event to celebrate an occasion, to share some typical past times and have pleasant conversations on points of interests for the team members.

Social intelligence not only happens face to face but also on the phone and through online media such as social forums internal and external to the organisations. These online forums also require social intelligence to take benefit of communication and shared goals. There are some ethical and moral dilemmas involved in social situations, especially in online forums. As it is in face to face social situations, politeness and courtesy are also vital principles to survive and thrive in social media.

Cultural diversity, inclusiveness, and privacy are some key concerns to be aware of in using online social media. Things can be quickly taken out of context with some careless remarks made with a rush and cause dilemmas to the social groups involved. Excellent leaders are aware of the consequences of a careless act in social media, and they become a role model by providing clear, precise and neutral communications at all times and show respect to others point of views and privacy.

In day to day interactions, excellent leaders with social intelligence are quite recognisable. People enjoy friendly approach posed by these excellent leaders. They are also outgoing yet courteous, tactful and diplomatic in their approach. These traits make excellent technical leaders outstanding in social situations. Event managers particularly look for these excellent leaders for social engagements.

Resourcefulness

Resourcefulness applies to maintain current good progress for the things working well, resolve ongoing issues for problematic areas, and create insights and new opportunities for growth. A resourceful technical leader can find creative ways to maintain working functions, deal with stressful situations, overcome challenges using well-formulated tactics, and at the same time have a strategic view for the growth, new insights, and generating new revenues.

Resourcefulness is closely related to leaders' knowledge, skills, capabilities, traits, and experiences in a broad spectrum of services and business models in organisations leading towards digital transformations. Some individual leadership characteristics, such as being mindful, energetic, uplifting, passionate, having emotional intelligence in dealing with people, having social intelligence, applying design thinking technics to visualise the goals, and many other such attributes can increase resourcefulness.

Resourceful technical leaders are capable of understanding the current situation, having a vision for the future state, articulating the needs to all stakeholders, and developing a pathway to reach the target state effectively using the talented team members who are following them. To this end for resourcefulness, excellent technical leaders are scarce resources and talents that organisations are aiming at technological transitions and digital transformations.

Prioritisation

Priority management, as opposed to time management, is a well-understood necessity for leaders. Excellent technical leaders manage their priorities rather than their time. Priority management is focusing on essential tasks which make a real difference for desired outcomes. Focusing on things that matter, avoiding distractions, removing roadblocks, creating enablers are fundamental characteristics of leaders to set the prioritisation for the digital transformation.

Excellent leaders don't complain about too much to do in too little time as they primarily focus on their priorities. Setting priorities, switching priorities and shuffling between priorities are the primary focus of their day to day work engagements for themselves and their followers. They ask whether something is essential to do now or can it wait. They take immediate actions to resolve an issue, to create a plan, to help a team member. By using this systematic action-oriented approach, nothing important accumulates; hence, they prevent any time management concerns.

Another essential technique they use to manage their priorities is to be able to delegate necessary actions to the right people in smart ways. The smart delegation not only allows them to free their times for other more critical duties but also it empowers the talented team members to engage and grow by undertaking additional duties and tasks.

Reaching Consensus

The consensus is an arrangement bringing all parties to an agreement for discussion of a topic, a matter or a problem to be solved. Consensus brings all parties on the same page and creates a win-win situation for all stakeholders. Excellent technical leaders are aware of this essential social necessity to create social productivity at work.

Reaching consensus for a large group of people requires exceptional communication skills, respect to others viewpoints, meaningful negotiations, pointing out blindspots respectfully, using precise definitions, articulation of details even more structurally and methodically, and providing logical representations of situations.

The excellent leaders employ various techniques to reach consensus. They can clarify rules of engagement for all parties, operating models in the organisation or departments, and underlying processes and procedures. Using these simple yet essential techniques when needed, can help the team members to reach consensus effectively on any circumstance and situation.

Effective Communicators

Excellent technical leaders are effective communicators. Effective communication is an inevitable aspect of leading people, dealing with situations effectively, and setting the strategies for transformations.

Effective communication requires unbiased listening, understanding others' point of views and conveying the message to the point in the right context. Clarity is one of the critical enablers of effective communication. Using the right words in the right context, refraining from jargons and ambiguous words are essential to effective communication.

Excellent leaders articulate the situations; however, they do not just trust the power of their communication, but they also find ways to validate the understanding of other people. More importantly, they follow up with team members and other stakeholders, whether the message is understood and appropriate actions are taken and in place.

Quick Learners

Learning is a lifelong process. Excellent technical leaders are self-learners in formal and informal settings. They already gained discipline from years of formal learning from schools and other formal learning environments. They also interact with people from day to day and participate in informal learning activities.

Every situation creates a learning opportunity for these leaders. Excellent technical leaders learn new situations quickly in the right context. They adjust themselves to the situations based on their capability to learn quickly, respond intelligently, and follow up efficiently.

In addition to learning, these excellent leaders are also great teachers. They pass their messages clearly and enable their followers to learn quickly. They use multiple senses and ways to convey their messages as they know that people have a different style of learning. More specifically, they try senses such as visual, audio, and tactile.

Quiet Achievers

Excellent technical leaders are known as quiet achievers. The term quite in this context is that they don't highlight their achievement and success overtly. Most of the time, they leave it to others to recognise and appreciate them rather than self-promoting their cases.

There may be a misconception about quiet achievers that they are introverts and may not talk much. Being introvert or extrovert is not directly related to this context. For example, quiet achievers may like listening more than talking. However, this doesn't mean that they are silent all the time. They only talk when needed with precision, context, brevity and impact.

Paradoxically there are extravert types of quiet achievers who don't like small talks but can do fantastic outstanding presentations such as public speaking for the points that they are passionate. They are confident to raise their hands and ask essential questions when needed in prominent public forms. However, they do not dominate or bog down conversations with their agendas.

Inspiring Others to Think

Leaders can make followers think in the right direction. They don't tell them what to do, how to do something, and when to do things, but they inspire them to think productively using various supportive techniques. Active listening and asking probing questions can help others think more clearly and effectively.

It is a subtle skill to make other people think. It is like the proverbial 'you can force a horse to a river but cannot make him drink'. This approach requires psychological knowledge and skilful refinement through years of working with people at various levels. Making other people think in the desired direction requires extensive psychological understanding.

As mentioned in earlier sections, emotional intelligence, social intelligence, and mindfulness are three of the necessary capabilities to inspire other people to think effectively. Paying attention to people's current moods, body language, tone of voice and other clues from their conversations, excellent leaders can steer conversations in healthier and productive ways.

This inspirational skills of excellent leaders can be useful for the team members during the problem-solving, performing complex analysis, making assessments, and critical decisions. Providing them with some clues, asking interesting questions, encouraging their thoughts, showing interest in what they were saying are useful techniques.

Influence

Leaders focus on the influence rather than power to cultivate creativity, make an impact on their goals, and desired outcomes. One of the primary influence areas for excellent technical leaders is related to the self-efficacy of team members. These leaders know that self-efficacy for their followers make a tremendous impact on the followers' performance, which can affect productivity positively in the workplace.

Influence requires several leadership characteristics and capabilities. One of the primary characteristics is building trust with people. Trust is believed to open all communication channels in the workplace. We open ourselves and show our authentic self to trusted leaders. Establishing the right trust is not easy, and it takes considerable time. Excellent technical leaders focus on creating trust with their team members. One of the related attribute and enabler of trust in the workplace is personal and professional integrity. Trust and integrity go hands in hands. Lacking integrity decreases or annihilates trust. When employers select technical leaders, one of the most fundamental aspect they look for is the integrity of the candidate.

Other essential attributes of creating influence on others are the consistency, reliability and principle centeredness of the leaders. Excellent technical leaders pay special attention to their behaviour to be consistent and aligned with the organisation's culture. They depict reliability by keeping their promises, acting reasonably, behaving assertively, and treating people fairly. Let's touch on principle centeredness in the next section.

Principle Centeredness

Principles are essential factors in all walks of life. Principles are fundamental truth and value propositions for systems, reasons, and behaviour. In my understanding, principle centeredness means to look at things based on truth. We set our principles and consistently adhere to them.

We accept principles as determining truth for our

conversations, actions, and interactions. It is useless to argue against principles because they are based on truth. We cannot change the truth whatever the cogent argument is posed. It is necessary for the technical leaders to utilise principles to influence their team members to reach their transformational goals.

Followers respect principle-centred leaders. These type of leaders reflect trust, reliability and integrity. Principle centred leaders behave ethically in all circumstances. They are transparent to the outside world. Their inner truth is reflected in their external actions and interactions. They don't compromise their integrity even when they face the direst situations.

Being a Catalyst

Being a catalyst means to cause an intentional change. This change can be for an event, a project, an initiative, or behaviour of people. Excellent technical leaders are change agents. They embrace change and influence others to change for their common goals.

These leaders create a meaningful sense of urgency to change people to better versions and situations to better conditions. They create compelling reasons which people cannot ignore and naturally collaborate to change.

Digital transformation certainly requires leaders as catalysts for change. Excellent technical leaders are ideal people who drive this change as a catalyst. They are the catalyst for every change, modification, iterations, and transitional activities comprising the overall transformation.

Self-Awareness and Self-Confidence

Self-awareness is knowing one's capabilities and

limitations. Self-awareness is also related to the term self-confidence. Self-aware leaders naturally have self-confidence. These two interrelated terms are essential characteristics of excellent leaders. The vital attributes of leaders are reflected in their day to day interactions with others.

One manifestation of this is that self-confident leaders take more calculated risks to create better opportunities. Self-aware and self-confident leaders connect better with other people. Since they are confident, their communication styles are noticeably bright and articulate. They are optimistic people, and they focus on good things to happen.

Self-confident leaders have a positive image of themselves. They also influence other people to be confident with them. They have self-assurance and self-esteem. These terms are all interrelated reflecting positive characteristics of excellent leaders.

Energy

Life is based on energy. Our energy is the fuel for us to survive and thrive in this world. Physical, mental and emotional energy is essential for leaders to shine. They know how to energise themselves at the right dose and right times. Their noticeable energy also inspires other people to gain energy to achieve their goals.

Excellent leaders exude positive emotions. Their positive emotions, especially passion and enthusiasm, are critical success factors to influence their followers and the people around them.

Energetic leaders are distinguishable in all walks of life. They deserve respect. They are influential and convincing for their passion points. Excellent technical leaders can create a sense of excitement for even the most mundane things in life by showing the interesting aspects stemming from their witty and bright minds.

The energy reflected by these leaders also helps people to see themselves in a more positive atmosphere. The followers can also visualise the futures described by these energetic leaders. They add energy to future events and conditions in people's mind. This is a fantastic opportunity to buy in for digital transformations.

However, the reality is showing that most of the leaders, especially technical leaders working in large corporations with complicated environments, face a substantial amount of stress diminishing or consuming their energy levels very quickly. The busy schedules and ongoing demands from multiple angles wear them out quickly.

Without energy, leaders have the risk of depicting lethargy. Lack of energy is the most undesirable situation for technical leaders. To this end, these leaders need to be mindful to look after themselves and balance their life to gain the required amount of energy to be successful in their endeavours.

Rejuvenating and gaining more energy are individual matters. Different people have different kinds of methods to deal with the stress of life. Excellent technical leaders are aware of these challenges, and they look after themselves carefully. They do it not only for themselves but for other people around them. They ensure that life-work balance is maintained in their teams.

Dealing with Distractions

Distractions are undesirable situations. They affect our productivity. Excellent leaders focus on their priorities and are capable of avoiding distractions. They recognise the distractions, especially hidden ones, and don't waste their energy on them.

Focusing on priorities naturally lowers the impact of distractions. Surrounded by technological devices may generate a considerable amount of distractions. Social media create substantial distractions. It is reported that a considerable percentage of workers use Facebook or other social media tools at work.

There are several other factors creating distractions in the workplace. For example, people's unreasonable demands may create distractions. Activities which have no value for the specific goals may create distractions. Leaders are aware of these types of distractions and stay away from these distractions and keep the team members focused on priority matters.

Trust and Integrity

Trust is essential for human interactions. We only deal with people with trust. If we don't trust a person, we stay away and keep our distance. No communication occurs when trust does not exist. Trust is essential in the workplace.

Trust opens the doors, but when there is no trust, nothing happens. Excellent leaders build trust on purpose using their multiple leadership and interpersonal skills. Their actions demonstrate trust. They refrain from action which may break the trust.

One of the vital enablers of trust is integrity. Excellent technical leaders create trust based on integrity. Trust and integrity are fundamental human traits which apply to all walks of life. Trust and integrity are crucial for leadership, especially in complex digital transformation areas.

Transparency and Openness

Being transparent means not having surprises, secret

agendas in the relationships and having clarity of thoughts for all parties. Technical leaders are open about their thoughts, views, ideas, vision, goals, and objectives. Excellent technical leaders openly share their goals with their teams and people around them in an inclusive way.

Openness also includes respecting other's views and opinions and embrace diversity in a team. They ensure that no one in their teams is discriminated or distanced based on their age, race, sex, look and other human traits.

They even encourage opposing views shared with respect. Embracing opposing views on things can be very useful for igniting creativity and innovation. Encouraging people out of the box and awarding them for the alternatives they generate for innovation.

Modesty and Humility

No one likes arrogant people; this is especially more important for leaders. People respect modest and humble leaders. Modest leaders take criticism as feedback, and they don't tend to punish who criticise them.

Modest leaders admit their mistakes with humility without self degrade. They embrace new ideas and don't resist their views as being superior to others. They refrain from dominating the conversations and discussion sessions.

Modesty attracts followers towards leaders. People feel at ease when they are around modest people. They know that their views and opinions can be taken seriously without being judged. Corporate cultures built on modesty and humility have stronger team relationships.

Interestingly, modest leaders are charismatic. People are attracted to modest leaders. Followers of these leaders feel comfortable around modest leaders. They open themselves with no fear or concern. They even find it as a therapeutic activity. This friendly and pleasant atmosphere created by modesty has a tremendous effect on productivity and success.

Charisma

We can define charisma as compelling attractiveness that can inspire devotion in leaders. Sometimes small things in life can generate attractiveness, which leads to charisma; for example, a genuine smile, a simple handshake, calling people with their names, correctly pronouncing foreign names are few to mention here.

In general, charismatic leaders are effective communicators — people like listening to them and follow them with passion. They hardly question their credibility as people are mesmerised by their gentle attitudes, engaging conversations and other pleasant characteristics.

Many attributes we pointed earlier, such as modesty, vision, persuasion, have a tremendous impact on creating charisma. Even though in general charisma is a personal thing, some aspects of it can be acquired and learned by following critical attributes of leadership. Two significant contributors to charisma can be emotional and social intelligence and mindfulness. Especially empathy aspect of mindfulness makes a significant impact on people.

Mindset

Our mindset reveals our personality. Mindset can be defined as a set of assumptions and beliefs one hold as their world view or personal trait. As Carol Dweck pointed out, people primarily have either a growth mindset or a fixed mindset. There are, of course, different mindsets in between reflecting different attributes of people.

Excellent technical leaders naturally have a growth

mindset rather than a fixed mindset. Leaders with a growth mindset are more resilient in life, more motivated, can deal with situations more effectively, develop better relationships, communicate more clearly, hence achieve better results.

These leaders have a desired transformational mindset to shift their organisations to better consumer experience, cleaner data, reliable infrastructure, well-functioning systems, secure environment, gaining insights, speed to market, and more transformational goals.

Other Pillars of Technical Leadership Framework

After introducing critical attributes of technical leadership excellence, we cover the remaining four pillars in this section. My aim here is to provide practical ideas on simplification, innovation, collaboration, and agility for empowering digital transformational leadership.

These fundamental pillars of technology leadership present established principles well-documented in the literature. Using these pillars, strategic technical leaders not only deal with known risks, but they also are expected to work on unknown unknowns. Even though predicting future events and circumstances are not easy, the technical leaders are equipped to take risks and mitigate them accordingly based on established principles covered under these pillars.

Technical or technology leaders in the digital arena have different job titles. The most common technical leadership roles are Chief Technology Officer, Chief Digital Officer, Chief Architect, Lead Enterprise Architect, Chief Information Officer, Principle Technical Consultant, Head of Technology. There are many more names, but this list enough for us to discuss and understand the typical responsibilities taken by these roles and expected an outcome from them.

These are senior technology roles recognised by many large organisations. It is widespread to see these roles in job advertisements. These senior technical roles usually well-paid and desirable roles which many technical professionals aim to be one in their career progression.

Now let's delve into characteristics, responsibilities and contributions of these technical leaders using our framework consist of five pillars in distinct chapters in the following sections.

Chapter Summary and Key Points

Excellence: Technical leaders strive for excellence rather than perfection. Excellence refers to having or demonstrating outstanding quality for the leaders for making a noticeable impact on other people, especially on the followers.

Uncertainty and Ambiguity: Technical leaders must demonstrate tolerance to uncertainty and ambiguity. Taking risk is one of the necessities and most fundamental characteristics of leaders for success.

Emotional Intelligence: Dealing with people and leading others require robust emotional intelligence. Emotional intelligence makes the leaders more self-aware with their fluctuating moods, changing emotions, and drives.

Mindfulness: Mindful leaders can cope with massive stress caused by hectic workplaces, volatile business situations, and ever-changing technologies effectively.

Personal Responsibility: Taking personal responsibility and being accountable for the situations technical leaders can leave better impressions on their followers. This positive disposition creates a trust for our integrity.

Actions: Excellent leaders are action-oriented. They prioritise their tasks and act immediately based on their priorities. They don't like delaying necessary actions. They dislike procrastination.

Vision: Leadership vision needs to display the values, beliefs, and culture of the organisation. Leaders' vision brings team members together; hence, they work for the same goals.

Social Intelligence: Interacting with people and feeling comfortable with many personalities is a core requirement of social intelligence. Socially intelligent leaders are outgoing yet courteous, tactful and diplomatic in their approach.

Resourcefulness: Resourceful technical leaders are capable of understanding the current situation, having a vision for the future state, articulating the needs to all stakeholders, and developing a pathway to reach the target state effectively using the talented team members who are following them.

Prioritisation: Priority management is focusing on essential tasks which make a real difference for desired outcomes. Focusing on things that matter, avoiding distractions, removing roadblocks, creating enablers are fundamental characteristics of leaders to set the prioritisation for the digital transformation.

Consensus: Technical leaders employ various techniques to reach consensus. They can clarify rules of engagement for all parties, operating models in the organisation or departments, and underlying processes and procedures.

Effective Communication: Effective communication requires unbiased listening, understanding others point of views and conveying the message to the point in the right context. Clarity is one of the critical enablers of effective communication. Using the right words in the right context, refraining from jargons and ambiguous words are essential to effective communication.

Fast Learning: Excellent technical leaders learn new situations quickly in the right context. They adjust themselves to the situations based on their capability to learn quickly, respond intelligently, and follow up efficiently.

Quiet Achievement: Excellent technical leaders are known as quiet achievers. They don't highlight their achievement and success overtly. Most of the time, they leave it to others to recognise and appreciate them rather than self-promoting their cases. They stand up when necessary.

Inspiring to Think: Paying attention to people's current moods, body language, tone of voice and other clues from their conversations, excellent leaders can steer conversations in healthier and productive ways.

Influence: Influence requires several leadership characteristics and capabilities. One of the primary characteristics is building trust with people. Trust built with integrity is believed to open all communication channels in the workplace.

Principles: We accept principles as determining truth for our conversations, actions and interactions. It is useless to argue against principles because they are based on truth.

A catalyst for Change: Technical leaders create a meaningful sense of urgency to change people and situations to better conditions.

Self Awareness and Confidence: Self-aware leaders naturally have self-confidence. Self-confident leaders take more calculated risks to create better opportunities. Self-aware and self-confident leaders connect better with other people. Their communication styles are noticeably bright and articulate. They are optimistic people, and they focus on good things to happen.

Energy: Physical, mental and emotional energy is essential for leaders to shine. They know how to energise themselves at the right dose and right times. Their noticeable energy also inspires other people to gain energy to achieve their goals.

Distractions: Technical leaders recognise the distractions, especially hidden ones, and don't waste their energy on them. Focusing on priorities naturally lowers the impact of distractions.

Trust and Integrity: Excellent leaders build trust based on integrity. These fundamental human traits, trust and integrity, apply to all walks of life and crucial for leadership in all domains.

Transparency: Technical leaders are transparent and open about their thoughts, views, ideas, vision, goals, and objectives. They even encourage opposing views shared with respect.

Modesty and Humility: Modest leaders admit their mistakes with humility without self degrade. They embrace new ideas and don't resist their views as being superior to others. They refrain from dominating the conversations and discussion sessions.

Charisma: In general, charismatic leaders are effective communicators — people like listening to them and follow them with passion. Followers hardly question the credibility of charismatic leaders as people are mesmerised by their gentle attitudes, engaging conversations and other pleasant characteristics.

Growth Mindset: Excellent technical leaders naturally have a growth mindset rather than a fixed mindset. Leaders with a growth mindset are more resilient in life, more motivated, can deal with situations more effectively, develop better relationships, communicate more clearly, hence achieve better results.

Chapter 3: Innovation

In this section, we start with understanding the importance of innovation as an empowering factor for digital transformation leadership. I attempt to provide my observations and thoughts on how excellent technical and technology leaders use innovation coupled with collaboration and principles of fusion-focused approach to initiate, empower, and deliver digital transformation goals. Let's start with defining innovation.

Definition of Innovation

We can define innovation in different terms based on the type of work, professions, industry, and other backgrounds. In this book, my definition of innovation is the use of creativity for generating new ideas, new methods, new approaches, new techniques, new processes, and new tools or improve the current environment to gain insights and business value.

Innovation is closely related to novelty, improvement, iterations, and ongoing steady progress. Innovative thinking generates novel ideas, focuses on improving ideas, and strives for making iterative progress.

Innovation and technical excellence are tightly coupled and interrelated. Innovation ignites technical excellence, and technical excellence enables innovation. Therefore, excellent technical leaders are natural innovators. They practice innovation in their daily life and motivate people around them to innovate.

Innovation feeds the culture and is a critical aspect of an ecosystem in organisations. Cultures embracing innovation can naturally renew themselves for surviving and thriving. They extend to the next generations with constant progress.

Innovative Thinking

Innovation starts with thinking differently. Innovative thinking requires multiple modes of thinking. Traditionally, most of us think vertically, linearly or in binary. We usually use vertical and linear types of thinking for problem-solving. Applying logic and streamlining thoughts are some techniques in this type of thinking mode. Linear thinking goes deep down, layer by layer, and in a logical manner. Binary thinking consists of simple terms such as yes or no, black and white, good or bad.

As opposed to vertical thinking, horizontal thinking covering more breadth rather than depth which was also coined as 'lateral thinking' by Edward de Bono is a type of thinking aiming to generate unpredictable ideas by breaking out the rigid thought patterns. Lateral thinking challenges the assumptions. It looks for alternatives and goes beyond the ordinary, creating radical solutions.

The horizontal type of thinking is beneficial for creating innovations. There are different techniques that we can use for horizontal thinking. Some commonly used techniques are randomisations, distortions, reversals, exaggerations, metaphors, analogies, dreaming, theme mining, questioning the norms, and creating contradictions.

One of the practical techniques that excellent technical leaders use is mind mapping. They articulate their thoughts using representative maps on paper or a whiteboard. They also use other visual representations, such as drawing pictures on a whiteboard while explaining abstract ideas. People can visualise abstract ideas better by looking at the drawings.

Innovation Culture and Ecosystem

Many technology organisations create an innovation

culture embedded in their organisation's ecosystem. The excellent leaders are the catalyst for the formation and maintenance of the innovation culture. With the support of their technical leaders, team members of these cultures continually challenge the status quo. People embrace changes and challenges in innovative cultures.

In these types of organisations, innovation becomes habitual. Team members strive for excellence by creating innovations in their day to day tasks. No one is called weird names or other judgemental adjectives. Instead, innovation is welcomed, praised, and even awarded in different ways. People embrace constant change, even if it is painful at times. They learn how to turn the pain to pleasure with the rewarding results of evident transformations.

People collaborate better in innovative cultures. They see themselves with the changing conditions in new positions. They do not resist as they know that change can be useful for them. In these innovative cultures, they have excellence centres or ideation labs. They perform ongoing trials and errors to create and test new ideas. They may fail at times, but they fail quickly and come back to reality with improved knowledge. They see the failing tests as new definitions.

Excellent technical leaders are catalysts for innovations. They support the innovative culture and water the innovation garden regularly to survive and thrive. They not only innovate but also enable others to innovate.

How to Ignite Innovation

Harnessing and driving creative thinking result in innovation. For excellent leaders, innovation turns to habit or more accurately a lifestyle. These leaders know the importance of innovation for digital transformation and inspire their followers to be innovative as well. The best way for these leaders to ignite innovation is to be a role model for their followers. They encourage the team members to innovate, and they reward them for their innovative achievements.

To ignite innovation, these leaders consider market conditions, client needs, and map them organisation's capabilities then define the focus areas for innovation agenda to enable digital transformation.

One of the methods they use is the design thinking activities which take place daily in the team interactions. Design thinking allows the team to be intuitive and logical at the same time. Design thinking enables team members to be more creative to recognise new patterns. As Design thinking is closely associated with the Agile methods, the design thinking professionals progress their ideas iteratively.

Innovation as a Mindset

Excellent leaders have a growth mindset to ignite innovation. They help their team members with a fixed mindset to convert to a growth mindset as it is an essential factor to survive and thrive in digitally transforming environments. Growth mindset leading towards innovation is a build-in characteristic in these technical leaders' personalities.

Metaphorically, it is like air and water for their survival. They also use innovation for thriving. They not only create innovation at a personal level but also through collaboration with their teams and extended teams. They keep asking how to deliver innovative experiences daily.

These leaders lead to a mindset shift in small and large teams. They hold a positive 'can do' attitude for any challenges they have. They are very customer-centric and put themselves in customers' shoes with strong empathy. Using design thinking techniques, they develop empathy maps.

They analyse the personas using empathy maps.

Blockers for Innovation

It is critical to recognise innovation blockers and show stoppers. The roadblocks to innovation can be from various angles. One of the main showstoppers is keeping the status quo. Traditional business processes are usually based on the status quo. There is a resistance to change in these cultures.

Even though the importance of innovation is well recognised in many organisations, there is always resistance towards innovation by some people who may have hidden agendas. It is essential for leaders to recognise those people who try to sabotage innovation. Even though they may be in the minority, they still may have a tremendous adverse impact on innovation in organisations.

One way of dealing with these innovation stoppers are to be transparent to them and have close conversations. Excellent technical leaders find ways to engage those types of people and show the value and benefit of innovation to these type of people. If those people can see the value for themselves, then they can be converted to innovation supporters. The critical point is asking them and making them think positively.

The business as usual mentality can be a roadblock for innovation. Cumbersome business processes and tired employees can hardly have any interest in innovation as they cannot see the immediate need. The best way is to separate innovation and business as usual as two different departments. Of course, business, as usual, is essential for the organisation to continue its current function but these organisations also need innovation for transforming to the digital world for new insights, market competitiveness, and revenue generation.

Chapter Summary and Key Points

Novelty: Innovation goes hand in hand with novelty, improvement, and ongoing progress. Innovative thinking generates novel ideas, focus on improving ideas, and strive for making iterative progress.

Culture: Innovation feeds the culture and is a critical aspect of an ecosystem in organisations. Cultures embracing innovation can naturally renew themselves for surviving and thriving. They extend to the next generations with constant progress. People collaborate better in innovative cultures. They see themselves with the changing conditions in new positions.

Horizontal Thinking: The horizontal type of thinking is beneficial for creating innovations. There are different techniques that we can use for horizontal thinking. Some commonly used techniques are randomisations, distortions, reversals, exaggerations, metaphors, analogies, dreaming, theme mining, questioning the norms, and creating contradictions.

Creative Thinking: Harnessing and driving creative thinking result in innovation. For excellent leaders, innovation turns to habit or more accurately a lifestyle.

Innovation Mindset: Excellent leaders have a growth mindset to ignite innovation. Growth mindset leading towards innovation is a build-in characteristic in these leaders' personalities.

Innovation Roadblocks: It is critical to recognise innovation blockers and show stoppers. The roadblocks to innovation can be from various angles. One of the main showstoppers is keeping the status quo.

Chapter 4: Simplicity

Simplicity is the next pillar in our framework. Simplicity is a substantial factor affecting digital transformations. Simplicity is also one of the critical attributes of excellent technical leaders. Simplicity touches almost every angle of transformation solutions. Therefore, I dedicated a chapter to highlight the importance and necessity of this pillar. Let's start exploring simplicity by defining it for a common understanding.

Meaning of Simplicity

Simplicity, related to excellence, is a paradoxical topic. One may ask how do you expect excellence to be provided with simplicity as excellence refers to complexity. Yes, excellence is a complex topic and require sophisticated attributes such as in-depth knowledge, varied skills, and extensive experience.

That's true! Ironically, to create simplicity, one needs to deal with a lot of complexity, complications and sophisticated matters. Obtaining the required knowledge, acquiring advanced skills, and gaining substantial experience are not easy and not indeed simple activities. Paradoxically, we need to deal with complexity to create simplicity.

However, one who deals with complexity and sophisticated matters can also have extraordinary attributes to simplify things for other people. We can call this simplicity for communication. Creating simplicity to communicate effectively with others is an essential leadership attribute.

Simplicity is a well sought-after characteristic in IT services and products. The digital world is formed for simplicity for consumers. As opposed to complexity, simplicity is favourable by consumers. Therefore, technical leaders are expected to simplify complex situations and complicated problems and offer simple solutions.

Excellent technical leaders can articulate the most complicated and complex matters in a simple format that is understandable by others. However, simplicity requires in-depth knowledge and flexible thinking. Simplicity also refers to clear communication. One way of clear communication is to customise our message to people's level and the right context we communicate.

Simplicity is a desired attribute not only for communication but also for dealing with technical matters and building relationships. Technical leaders communicate in simple terms. They can simplify technical matters when dealing with technical issues. They establish relationships that depict simplicity and efficiency.

User-centric excellent leaders ask the question of how they can create products and services simple, intuitive, and human-centric. The consumer-oriented simplicity is a requirement for leading innovative teams. They motivate their teams to think in simple terms when conveying complicated technical processes.

The path to digital transformation begins with simplifying the technology and process components at all levels. One of the effective ways to this simplification is automating routine tasks and technology stacks. Automation can help to simplify. Excellent technical leaders, while delving into details in technology, they also focus on emerging needs by simplifying them in consumer terms.

Process Simplicity

Consumers keep complaining that technology creates complexity and make it difficult to understand concepts and objects in natural human language. For example, many consumers complain about the cumbersome documentation written in a convoluted language. They also show their disapproval for voluminous of documents for the use of a small technology device. They call it a waste.

There is a generational disconnect in dealing with process simplicity. The old generation used to read manuals to solve their computer problems. Software stacks used to come large read-me files. However, the new generation works with technology intuitively. They hardly look at a product manual. If they are stuck, they would usually watch a YouTube video on how to do something or how to troubleshoot something. Instead of reading, they prefer watching a video. This is a dramatic cultural shift in consumer technologies.

Excellent technical leaders have a mission to simplify the business and technology processes and make them user-centric. This effort aims at efficiency and effectiveness of technology product and services leading to digital transformation.

Service Simplicity

Technology is rapidly transforming towards service orientation. Most of the technology domains are provided based on services models. The most common technology trend is the Cloud services model. In the Cloud services model, everything is provided as services such as infrastructure as a service, platform as a service, software as a service and many other technology stacks as a service.

The services model requires substantial amounts of simplification for users to take benefits of using technologies. Technical leaders using their skills to simplify services can add value to the business. They inspire and motivate their followers to simplify everything by empathising with consumers. Simplification is an innovative process that excellent leaders lead as role models.

Simplicity and clarity are closely related. Especially in the technical services industry, providing a transparent experience to the technical team members can be very beneficial. Besides, making this transparent experience available to the end-user even more simplified and more explicit formats for the usage patterns can add additional value to the service provision goals.

The best way of providing simplicity to the consumer is to think like the consumers. Excellent technical leaders keep focusing on the core tenets of simplifying products and services for the best possible user experience and satisfactory consumption merits.

Design Simplicity

Design simplicity is an essential factor to consider in services models. The simplicity in design can be reflected in delivering services and supporting underlying systems.

Applying design thinking, combined with adopting agile methods for design, is one of the simplification approaches. Simplification is an enabler for agile service delivery. Agile methods strive for simplifications using an iterative approach. Iterations are simpler than whole chunks.

By applying agile methods to the design phase, complicated requirements are simplified using simple use cases based on personas. Complex systems are deconstructed to smaller parts and dealt with simpler chunks. System relationships are simplified with iterative flows. The focus is on smaller building blocks.

Most of the technology services nowadays are digitally offered using mobile devices such as tablets and smartphones. Mobile designs must focus on simplicity by removing clutter from screens due to the nature of small screen views. These types of designs must focus on only fundamentally essential objects.

At technical matters, designing complex systems also require simplifications through modular and service-oriented designs. Modularity and modular approaches to complex solutions are essential for simplification and digital transformation. One of the approaches can be a domain-based walkthrough of simplifying modules of IT infrastructure, applications, architecture, middleware, security, network, and data domains. For example, in Big Data solutions and ecosystems, it is desirable to have a simplified schema for the databases.

To elaborate on design simplification, let's take containers as an example. Containers break down monolithic interdependent architectures into manageable, and independent components. A container, as a loosely coupled system, is an entire runtime environment in a bundle. It includes dependencies, binaries, libraries, and configuration files. These new techniques and approaches help us simplify the design process.

Excellent technical leaders are conscious of simplicity for design. They run workshops to convey the message for the intuitive user-centric designs based on simplicity principles.

Simplicity of Specifications

For many years, time and energy spent on the system and user specification of software and hardware products and services were substantial. There cost an enormous amount of funds for the projects developing the specifications with many talented engineers, technical architects and other technical specialists. However, it became evident that the investment made on these specifications yielded in little gain than expected.

The digital trends, mobile culture and agile approaches made substantial changes in addressing the cumbersome specifications, especially concerning the users or consumers. The deep-down technical details for user specifications were found unnecessary. An interesting approach was proposed by Agile methods and gained attention over a decade now. Agile methods proposed simplifications of cumbersome specifications in user stories format.

User stories are simple templates, including the functionalities, capabilities, and specifications from users or consumers point of view. Developing and understanding the user stories consist of a page or so are much more comfortable and more effective than developing or reading hundreds of pages of specifications in traditional methods.

Simplicity in Technical Communication

Effective communication requires simplification. Technical leaders are capable of simplifying communication. The simplification process for communication enables to facilitate understanding of issues, risks and dependencies effectively. Simplified communication is a challenging task, but we can apply it to our day-to-day interactions by using specific rules and techniques. These leaders can translate complex problems into clear messages that can be acted on, execute with simplicity and agility.

Refraining from convoluted phrases and instead, use of precise language is an essential factor in simplifying communication. Even though technical leaders have an extensive vocabulary, particularly in-depth knowledge of technical terms, they are capable of using simple language to pass their message to non-technical people's level. For example, they use different terms and references while speaking to a manager, a secretary, an executive, a salesperson, and a technician.

While they are using advanced business terms to senior executives to articulate a point, they can use deep technical terms to talk with engineers or technical specialists. This awareness, customisation, and flexibility in communication is a crucial characteristic of technical leaders.

The attention span for our generation is relatively low due to many technical disruptions in our lives. Technical leaders must get the point quickly before losing the attention of people. For example, they may use lively words to illustrate a situation rather than using abstract terms.

Simplicity in written communication is essential too. People don't have much time and brainpower to understand intricate details in a technical document. The authors must be sharp and to the point with clear statements. Short sentences are always preferable to improve readability.

The main benefit of simplification for oral and written communication is to pass the desired message effectively in the shortest possible time. It is beneficial to refrain from jargons, big words and complex sentence structures in oral and written communication.

Being able to articulate a situation in the simplest possible terms also can increase the confidence of the target person when dealing with the technical leader.

The right context in simplifying the language is also required. It is essential to balance qualitative and quantitative aspects while conveying a message to the audience. Excellent technical leaders are context-aware, and they deliver their message in the right context.

In their day to day relationships with the business stakeholders, excellent technical leaders strive to articulate the business value proposition rather than showing off their technical eminence detailing convoluted details.

Governance Simplicity

Complex and complicated governance processes and procedures can be a hurdle for digital transformation. They can cause delays, confusions, rework and low performance for the transformation initiatives. Therefore, it is critical to simplify governance framework, process and procedures for digital transformation.

Excellent technical leaders know the importance of governance and pay special attention to the required rigour. They do not compromise the quality requirements in governing technology solutions. However, while having this rigour, they also have a balance for delivering the message in the simplest possible terms and making the processes for governance in the most effective ways.

These leaders are staying on top of technology trends and developments to govern them. As part of their governance role, they ensure all technology practices adhere to regulatory standards in their industries.

The paradox of Data Simplification

Data simplification is a widely discussed topic in all IT environments. One way of simplifying data is to clean data, remove duplications and errors. Reducing data sources and volumes when needed are also used to simplify data management processes.

However, there is a paradoxical situation to point out for data volumes as far as simplicity is concerned. For example, more data is believed to create complexity; however, this is not true. It is just the opposite situation. Since we have more data to feed the system, the system can be more straightforward with rich data.

The simplicity can be achieved through the right data analysis, intelligence, powerful tools, and effective management strategies. In other words, when correctly and purposefully analysed, more data can add better intelligence.

Excellent technical leaders knowing the importance of data for digital transformations and using the established techniques and evolving methods in data science can leverage the industry knowledge and strive for simplifying data collection, process, management, storage and analytics.

Besides, for digital transformations, the traditional data management methods cannot suffice; therefore, they need to consider Big Data management technologies, process and tools for this simplification process.

One of the simplified Big Data trends in massive digital transformation initiatives is the use of Cloud services for Big Data solutions. There is even a specific Big Data as a Service model. For more information on this topic, you can check my book Architecting Big Data Solutions Integrated with IoT and Cloud available in digital and paper copies.

Simplified Presentations for Effectiveness

Dead from PowerPoint is a famous statement made in all online forums depicting inefficiencies of presentations using tools like PowerPoint. Being brief and concise in presentations is also an essential simplification method for effective communication. For example, we can simplify team presentations by cutting unnecessary, irrelevant details and using a concise number of slides focusing on necessary points when using a PowerPoint as a tool.

Another crucial consideration is focusing on conveying the intended central message rather than trying to impress the audience with sophisticated communication techniques. Endless discussions may cloud the essential message; therefore, it is critical to control the presentation process and focus sharply on the essential points in our presentations.

Excellent technical leaders provide simplified, clear and concise presentations without compromising the quality of content and effectiveness of the message. They also encourage the team members to follow simplicity principles in their presentations and provide constant constructive feedback to maintain this simplicity culture.

Chapter Summary and Key Points

Complexity versus Simplicity: Ironically, to create simplicity, one needs to deal with a lot of complexity, complications and sophisticated matters. Obtaining the required knowledge, acquiring advanced skills, and gaining substantial experience are not easy and not indeed simple activities. Paradoxically, we need to deal with complexity to create simplicity.

Consumer-Oriented Simplicity: User-centric excellent leaders ask the question of how they can create products and services simple, intuitive, and human-centric. The consumer-oriented simplicity is a requirement for leading innovative teams.

Process Simplicity: Simplifying processes are critical. Consumers keep complaining that technology creates complexity and make it difficult to understand concepts and objects in natural human language.

Services Simplicity: The services model requires substantial amounts of simplification for users to take benefits of using technologies. Service simplification is essential for digital transformation and adds substantial value to the business from every angle.

Design Simplicity: Applying design thinking, combined with adopting agile methods for design, is one of the simplification approaches.

The simplicity of Specifications: The digital trends,

mobile culture and agile approaches made substantial changes in addressing the cumbersome specifications, especially concerning the users or consumers. The deep-down technical details for user specifications were found unnecessary. Agile methods proposed simplifications of cumbersome specifications in user stories format.

Simplicity in Technical Communication: The simplification process for communication is essential and enables to facilitate understanding of issues, risks and dependencies effectively. The right context in simplifying the language is also required. It is essential to balance qualitative and quantitative aspects while conveying a message to the audience.

Governance Simplicity: Complex and complicated governance processes and procedures can be a hurdle for digital transformation. They can cause delays, confusions, rework and low performance for the transformation initiatives. Therefore, it is critical to simplify governance framework, process and procedures for digital transformation.

Data Simplicity: simplicity can be achieved through the use of accurate data analysis, intelligence, effective management strategies, and powerful tools. In other words, when correctly and purposefully analysed, more data can add better intelligence.

Chapter 5: Agility

Agility is our next pillar in this framework. Technology leaders in this era must be agile to be influential, competitive, and productive in their fields. Digital transformation leaders keep asking how they can make their IT footprint more intuitive, responsive, and agile day today. Whist dealing with legacy IT footprint in an agile manner, these leaders also have the vision of well-functioning modernisation and put their energies on rapid-paced digital transformations.

It is almost impossible to succeed with old methods as many organisations adapted to agility and matured in delivering rapidly. Agility is a particular concern for digital transformations as consumer demands are increasing based on fast-paced delivery requirements.

Speed to market is one of the most fundamental requirements of businesses nowadays. Agile became the new norm in technology organisations. Products are expected to be released faster than they were in the past. Security updates and bug fixes are required more frequently.

Agility affects all aspects of transformation. Besides, technical leaders are expected to act, behave and approach in agility to every aspect of the digital transformation solutions. We cover various aspects of agility in the subsequent sections. Let's start with the communication of agility.

How to Communicate Agility

Selling agile is reasonably easy due to its nature and compelling reasons. Agile is a particular interest to the new generations as they grow with agility in all walks of life. However, the older generation still has a sentimental attachment to waterfall methods. There appears to be some comfort zone created for using waterfall methods.

There is a common perception that Agile methods cut things short hence reduce the quality; however, this is not true. Some agile projects increase the quality due to iterative approaches and checking quality more frequently in every milestone.

Excellent technical leaders articulate the benefits and compelling reasons to use the Agile approach, especially for digital transformations. It is not feasible to wait and see the end of a gigantic digital transformation project. Ther are so many unknowns; hence, it is not possible to see the end product without trial and error.

An agile approach allows the team members to test their ideas iteratively. If they fail, they fail quickly and cheaply without costing lots of funds to the initiatives. This business value needs to be understood well and needs to be embedded in the culture of the organisations striving for digital transformations. Excellent technical leaders are the catalyst for conveying the message and making the necessary cultural adjustments effectively.

How to Ignite and Maintain Agility

Excellent leaders ignite agility as being motivators. As they are technically capable and business-focused, they show the value and share their knowledge and views with team members and other stakeholders.

These leaders actively participate in Agile scrums and provide ongoing feedback and support to the teams. These leaders can also perform the role of the product owner in Agile scrums. As product owners, they set the acceptance criteria for the product in the digital transformation sprint.

These excellent leaders develop mental models on how technology users interact with their solution in each iteration. With their action-oriented approach, they use the backlogs quickly and in priority orders. In addition, these leaders use rewards and recognise the high achievers' effort and contributions for clearing the backlogs in the most effective and innovative ways.

Pragmatic Architecture

Based on my many years of experience as an Enterprise Architect, architecture creates fear for the organisations due to valid reasons. In the simplest terms, architecture involves things that are hard to change later. However, this doesn't mean we cannot apply agile to architecture. There is a massive trend to use Agile methods for developing architectural solutions.

Transformational leaders take a pragmatic approach to architecture development. We know that predicting the future is very hard; therefore, creating an upfront paragon of architecture is not practical. We cannot afford the use of Waterfall methods for developing architectures for many months and even years. Taking this extended time is not feasible in this digital age. Consumers expect product and services much quicker than old times.

An iterative approach to architecture can be the most effective investment in the earlier stages of the digital transformation. We can see the architecture development like product development. The iterative method can speed up the architectural process and improve the quality based on the minimally viable product development approach.

Rapid Development

After architecture and design, another big topic and concern is development. By using waterfall methods developing a software product used take months and years in the past. Again, consumers cannot wait this long any more. The solution is applying an Agile approach to development.

Fortunately, Agile methods are more suited to the development areas.

There are many evolving Agile methods to support different kinds of development processes. Developers embrace Agile methods. They can see the results much more quickly. Use of evolving methods such as DevOps is also prime considerations for enabling digital transformations.

Excellent leaders focus on rapid development and deployment of flexible solutions using Agile methods. They are mindful that speedy time-to-market for digital products is a competitive differentiator in this day and age.

Automate As Much As Possible

Transforming to digital services and delivering products fast to market requires substantial automation activities. Agile methods have a particular focus on automation. Automation enables simplifying and speeding up processes.

Excellent leaders understand the value of automation, and they know that through automation, they can reduce the number of resources required to maintain manual and tedious systems. Automation can address human errors and resolve potential errors in an effective way. People in agile cultures do not resist against automation, in fact, they embrace it.

These leaders with particular focus on automation move people to more value-adding roles rather than performing repetitive and boring tasks that computers can undertake. People focusing on stimulating and high-value items also tend to create more innovative solutions.

Remove Silos

Silos are proven to slow the whole life cycle, from

architecting, designing and developing, marketing and selling products and services. They also impact the quality of the products due to a lack of integrated view in siloed cultures. Departments in silos may not know each other's progress and cause some duplicate of works or rework. They may not produce a single integrated product or services to the consumers. Some departments in these traditional settings in the same organisations even compete with each other. What an undesired situation!

Agility approach requires moving from silos to a flatter structure to resolve the issues of isolated and hierarchical structures in large organisations. Excellent leaders following the agile method pay special attention to collaboration, co-locations, and face to face teamwork rather than having silos and hierarchies.

These leaders continuously deal with culture and ecosystem implications. They strive to break silos, instead of coming above, they create flat structures, resulting in collaborative self-managing teams with many domain experts as peers.

Manage your Backlog Effectively

Maintaining backlogs in agile methods are critical. Excellent technical leaders make day to day management of backlogs in a priority order a habit. They manage their team's backlog effectively. Even if they perform the role of a scrum master or a product owner, these technical leaders keep the team members accountable for their backlog items.

Since these leaders know the importance of prioritisation, they continuously focus on the priority items and deal with the backlog items based on their priority orders. Their backlogs run very efficiently and productively. Backlog management is a critical factor of digital transformation sprints.

Priority is set by using various considerations. One of the critical aspects is the creation of a minimum viable product using the Agile method. A Sprint is the shortest time bombed duration to create the minimum viable product. Consumer expectations, financial constraints, resource issues, and business priorities all have an impact on setting priorities for clearing backlogs.

Embrace Change

Agile methods mandate change. Change management is a vital aspect of Agile methods. Embracing change is critical to be successful in agile delivery. Adapting to constant change is very important for agility.

Managing every user story, clearing a backlog item and running a Sprint is all about constant change. Dealing with this constant change requires flexibility and agility in designing, developing and implementing agile solutions.

Technical leaders and their followers engaged in agile processes and solutions embrace the constant change. They become the change agents. The digital transformation certainly needs such a change-oriented agile approach.

Fail Fast

One of the benefits of using agile methods come from the iterative approach. In other words, we tackle solutions in smaller chunks with agility. Agile methods enable the principles of the fail fast, fail early, fail cheaply.

Of course, failure is not for the sake for failure, no one enjoys failure, but it is beneficial to fail earlier than later to keep the cost of failure low and be successful in the long run from the lessons learnt from small failures.

Even though it is called 'fail fast' it refers to constant

trial and error to deal with unknowns in a fast and effective way. Learnings from these trial and errors constitute the progress for designing, developing and implementing complex solutions.

Cost and Revenue Relationship with Agility

In business, we can consider every resource and effort as a cost. Even though technical leaders are well paid and costing business for their salaries, as they are cost-aware and know how to reduce cost, they make their projects profitable, generate more revenue, especially delivering with agility. They focus on increasing efficiencies and lowering costs.

Agile is a cost-focused and revenue-generating approach. Technical leaders can manage costs better and generate more revenue by adopting agile approaches in high impact tasks and solution development activities in their organisations. Through incremental progress, prioritised backlog management, speedy iterative delivery through Sprints, the cost of failure for big chunks of work items can be prevented, and costs can be turned into revenues in a productive way.

Excellent technical leaders are capable of turning costs to investment. Due to their vision, innovative approaches and agile delivery, the costs incurred from the initiatives of these leaders can be seen as an investment. Investment on excellent technical leaders generate new businesses and bring substantial revenues with their contributions both at tactical and strategic levels.

Chapter Summary and Key Points

Market demand: Technology leaders in this era must be agile to be influential, competitive and productive in their fields. It is almost impossible to succeed with old methods as many organisations adapted to agility and matured in delivering rapidly. Besides, consumer demands increased substantially.

Generational Gap: Agile is a particular interest to the new generations as they grow with agility in all walks of life. However, the older generation still has a sentimental attachment to waterfall methods.

Maintain Agility: These excellent leaders develop mental models on how technology users interact with their solution in each iteration. With their action-oriented approach, they use the backlogs quickly and in priority orders.

Pragmatic Architecture: architecture involves things that are hard to change later. However, this doesn't mean we cannot apply agile to architecture. There is a massive trend to use Agile methods for developing architectural solutions.

Agile Development: There are many evolving Agile methods to support different kinds of development processes. Developers embrace Agile methods. They can see the results much more quickly. Use of evolving methods such as DevOps is also prime considerations for enabling digital transformations.

Automation: Agile methods have a particular focus on automation. Automation enables simplifying and speeding up processes.

Removing Silos: Agility approach requires moving from silos to a more flat structure to resolve the issues of isolated and hierarchical structures in large organisations.

Minimum Viable Product: Priority is set by using various considerations. One of the critical aspects is the creation of a minimum viable product using the Agile method. A Sprint is the shortest time bombed duration to create the minimum viable product.

Embracing Change: Agile methods mandates change. Change management is a vital aspect of Agile methods. Embracing change is critical to be successful in agile delivery. Adapting to constant change is very important for agility.

Failing Fast: Agile methods enable the principles of the fail fast, fail early, fail cheaply. Of course, failure is not for the sake for failure, no one enjoys failure, but it is beneficial to fail earlier than later to keep the cost of failure low and be successful in the long run from the lessons learnt from small failures.

Cost and Revenue: Agile is a cost-focused and revenue-generating approach. Technical leaders can manage costs better and generate more revenue by adopting agile approaches in high impact tasks and solution development activities in their organisations. Through incremental progress, prioritised backlog management, speedy iterative delivery through Sprints, the cost of failure for big chunks of work items can be prevented, and costs can be turned into revenues in a productive way.

Chapter 6: Productive Collaboration & Fusion

This section provides an overview of collaboration from a productivity angle. Collaboration is also important to extend to fusion principles. We need to define these terms to reach a common understanding.

Once we establish a common understanding of productive collaboration and fusion consecutively, then we can explore how these characteristics help the leaders excel in their transformational goals, improve day to day duties, and make them excellent leaders.

Let's start with the definition of collaboration.

Defining Collaboration

Collaboration may mean different things to different people. It is an overused term, especially with the emergence of internet technologies called collaborative tools, especially in a social media context.

In simple terms, we can define collaboration as a team of people working together for mutual goals. The team and mutual goals are essential entities of this simple framework. We should also focus on the work aspect of the collaboration rather than entertainment or hobbies.

Collaboration may take place in different modes and formats. One example is two or more people sharing ideas for a project plan. People may also collaborate by writing using various documentation tools such as Box, Google docs, or network version of Microsoft Office products. There are also emerging tools mainly used in mobile settings, usually in Agile methods such as Slack, Trello, Twitter, Facebook

Messenger, and many more.

Social media tools are touted as useful and highly valuable for collaboration purposes. However, when these tools examined carefully, we can see that they are more information-sharing tools rather than actual collaboration tools.

Collaboration is an essential tool for excellent leaders to create outstanding results. These leaders collaborate widely and productively. They also motivate their followers to collaborate effectively and efficiently by pointing out the common goals and making them compelling for collaboration.

Fusion for Collaboration

The term fusion refers to joining different things with different attributes or functions together to create a single new entity or form. The notion of fusion relates to concepts such as integration, blending, merging, amalgamation, and bonding. Fusion is closely related to collaboration from several angles. It is a kind of particular collaboration type designed for specific and advanced missions.

Fusion principles aim to bring individuals from various backgrounds, small groups with different purposes, various teams with differing capabilities, communities of practices with different missions under a single umbrella for serving a mission.

This is the most advanced and effective type of collaboration especially required for complex and complicated digital transformation initiatives with unique goals and market focus due to its powerful effects. Creating fusion-based collaboration can be very challenging. Technical leaders with extensive technical and people skills and experiences can create fusion-based collaboration.

How to ignite and enable collaboration

There are different ways to enable collaboration. Technical leaders usually take the responsibility to initiate them. These leaders are passionate for their goals, and they don't wait for collaboration to happen by itself. They know that nothing can happen by itself. Naturally, someone with leadership skills must initiate it. This action focus on collaboration is one of the outstanding characteristics of strategic technical leaders. They are typically extrovert people.

Once they initiate collaborative activities and invite their collaborators, then the process is maintained with necessary communication and engagement rules. Effective communication is a critical enabler of collaboration. Depending on the medium, both verbal and written communication types are essential for collaboration to happen.

Collaboration for co-located teams are usually conducted on face to face and can primarily be dynamic in delivery. However, geographically distant teams usually use video conferencing, telephone, chat programs, email or some agile collaboration tools. In remote teams, written communication is critical. Written communications can create some challenges, such as a careless piece of writing may cause some offence and kill the spirit of collaboration. Therefore, excellent technical leaders play an essential role in facilitating these types of communication by moderating the communication channels.

How to maintain collaboration

Once the collaboration is initiated and enabled, it needs to be maintained to be able to have the desired outcomes. Excellent technical leaders need to create the necessary process and procedures to main the collaboration.

Even though they set the initial team and processes to support the team activities, it is also the responsibilities of other team members to contribute to the goals set by these collaborative plans. To this end, excellent leaders also take the role of motivators to keep the team inspired by showing their impactful vision and strategic goals.

By focusing on productive collaboration at various levels, these leaders leverage insights from cross-functional teams and community of practices to create differentiated value propositions for the digital transformation.

Magic of Collaboration

By undertaking many tasks to initiate and maintain collaboration, the strategic technical leaders keep repeating these activities multiple times with multiple teams and integrate these teams to aggregate collaboration. The magic of collaboration starts with these repetitions. Successful repetitions make ripple effects for more success. In a relatively short time frame, these teams create a collaborative culture aligned with the organisation's ecosystem and strategic goals.

This collaborative culture at work can be invaluable. When collaborative culture starts flourishing using fusion-based collaboration, a desirable phenomenon called innovation happens naturally. Collaboration and innovation are tightly coupled processes.

Innovation is one of the exciting results provided by a collaborative culture with diversity, inclusiveness and implementation of fusion approach. The power of connected people from diverse backgrounds for the same goal generates new ideas and insights. Some of these ideas and insights may touch people from different angles and further motivate them even to take more responsibilities in this ecosystem. This shift causes the emergence of new leaders with the ignition of the initial strategic technical leader. Innovation generating collaborative culture is highly desirable for creating new business and growing established businesses.

This magical aspect of collaboration causing innovation is an ideal situation for digital transformations. Excellent technical leaders take advantage of this desirable situation by creating, maintaining, facilitating and further improving.

Importance of influence for Collaboration

Influence is an essential leadership attribute. It is particularly essential for collaboration. Technical leaders influence their collaborators with their responsibility, accountability, and demonstrated credibility.

Credibility in technical environments is critical. Technical leaders must be credible. These leaders earn the trust of their collaborators with credibility and integrity. Strategic technical leaders pay special attention to remain credible in their fields.

When we establish trust, another magic happens. People start sharing their true selves. They become more productive and more creative. Transforming people to show their true selves is another desirable situation in a collaborative culture.

Importance of Diversity for Collaboration

Diversity is a critical factor in creating collaborative teams and inclusive cultures. Diversity is extra critical for digital transformation due to the require creativity and innovation by people from different backgrounds, skills sets and experiences.

Trust is a requirement for diversity. Only with trust and trusted environments, people can show their true identities. When people start showing their true self, a diverse culture starts flourishing. Diversity is an enhancer of collaboration.

More importantly, with diversity, also innovation pops up stronger and faster. Diverse ideas ignite and accelerate innovation. With this approach, new options and choices are created. Connecting those choices and options also make a ripple effect on the culture.

Chapter Summary and Key Points

Collaboration: we can define collaboration as a team of people working together for mutual goals. The team and mutual goals are essential entities of this simple framework. We should also focus on the work aspect of the collaboration rather than entertainment or hobbies.

Fusion: Fusion principles aim to bring individuals from various backgrounds, small groups with different purposes, various teams with differing capabilities, communities of practices with different missions under a single umbrella for serving a mission.

Initiating Collaboration: Once they initiate collaborative activities and invite their collaborators, then the process is maintained with necessary communication and engagement rules. Effective communication is a critical enabler of collaboration.

Magic of Collaboration: The magic of collaboration starts with these repetitions. Successful repetitions make ripple effects for more success. In a relatively short time frame, these teams create a collaborative culture aligned with the organisation's ecosystem and strategic goals.

Influence for Collaboration: Technical leaders influence their collaborators with their responsibility, accountability and demonstrated credibility. They earn the trust of their collaborators. Strategic technical leaders pay special attention to remain credible in their fields.

Diversity: Diversity is an enhancer of collaboration. More importantly, with diversity, also innovation pops up again. Diverse ideas ignite innovation.

Chapter 7: Roles & Responsibilities

In this section, we explore the vital roles and responsibilities of technology leaders and excellent technical leaders in complex and complicated digital transformation environments. We call them roles and responsibilities, but some of them can be understood as activities. These are not job roles or position titles but help us to recognise the excellent technical leaders from their day to day activities and interactions. Let's start with technical eminence.

Technical Eminence

Technical eminence refers to outstanding technical expertise recognised internally and externally to the organisation of a technical leader who is influential and high impact to both technical and business communities.

Technical eminence requires not only expertise in technical areas but also all associated and related domains in a broader scope. Eminent leaders have strong industry skills, thought leadership, and multiple domain expertise. They are highly regarded and sought after for their views and contributions.

Excellent technical leaders referred in this book need to demonstrate technical eminence. Leading and motivating talented technical team members for successful digital transformation initiatives require to become an eminent leader in multiple technology domains with deep and broad understanding. Technical eminence is a prerequisite role for excellent technical leaders.

Communicators

Exceptional communication skills are essential for excellent technical leaders. Their communication skills are well respected and sought after. Excellent technical leaders can communicate at all levels with confidence and ease.

They also encourage other people to communicate clearly and effectively to share their knowledge in the team or outside of the immediate teams. These leaders are communication mentors and coaches. They observe their team members and provide constructive feedback for their growth.

Excellent technical leaders can articulate complex and complicated technologies to both technical people in necessary details and succinctly to the businesspeople using the right terms and references for clarity.

Innovators and Inventors

Technology leaders are innovators. They are original thinkers. These leaders continuously combine and contrast things to create new meanings, new understandings, new use cases, and new values.

To some extent, these leaders are also inventors. They look at the things from a novelty perspective. These leaders create new values for old concepts, terms or ideas. They look at things from different angles.

These leaders understand the value of innovation, they can become a catalyst for innovation, and they keep innovating. Excellent technical leaders create an innovation culture and embed it to the organisations' ecosystem. We cover innovative aspects of these leaders in a separate chapter in this book.

Mentoring and Coaching

Excellent technical leaders mentors their team members, other team members, people from partnering organisations, students from universities, and even external people in other organisations.

These leaders are also good at coaching their peers, subordinates, and cross-team members by being a soundboard to them. They are excellent listeners and even contribute to well being of their team members providing coaching sessions resulting in therapeutic outcomes.

They also provide technical mentorship to other executives who are not as technologically savvy. Their mentoring and coaching capabilities help their team members to stretch themselves to bigger and better roles. They can coach team members as one on one basis or in groups.

Change Catalyst

Change is critical for digital transformation. Everything changes continuously and rapidly. Change management is a vital function. Dealing with this rapid change is not an easy task, and indeed require delicate skills, experience, and insights.

These excellent technical leaders are catalysts for change. With their catalytical contributions, they refresh the culture to a more agile, collaborative, and innovative landscape.

These leaders create new sets of practices in the ecosystem. Their attributes, such as being responsive, sharing and learning mutually, and having fun with joy in a pleasant team environment, can have a tremendous impact on improving the culture.

Active Learners

Learning is a never-ending process in transformational environments. Due to changing technologies, process and tools, leaders and their followers need to learn rapidly and efficiently.

Excellent technical leaders can have a wide variety of learning styles. Based on situations and conditions, they can learn formally and informally. They turn every possible interaction to a potential learning opportunity.

These leaders can create learning opportunities for themselves and their team members. They can also teach other people actively and on-demand. By teaching their team members, they even learn more and better.

Keeping Talent

Talent is essential in digital transformation solutions. No talent, no transformation, it is this simple. Therefore, excellent technical leaders understand the value and importance of talent for digital transformations.

These leaders are very cautious to keep talent. They make every effort not to lose any talent from their teams. Talent is one of the critical enablers of core products and services of transforming organisations. Without talent, an organisation cannot be competitive in digital transformations.

These leaders also perform talent management and facilitation roles. They encourage the employees to perform better and turn them into talented team players. These leaders can also pick up poor performance in the team and help remove poorly performing employees and replace them with talented team members.

Building High-Performance Team

Digital transformations require team members who can perform at the highest possible level. We can call it optimally performing team members too. These are selected employees. Their skills and capabilities were tested and validated to suit the type of work they are performing.

Building high-performance teams are critical for technical leadership. Excellent technical leaders create collaborative, well functioning, and high performing teams to run successful digital transformation initiatives.

These leaders create proactive and engaged local technical teams and community of practices. These high-quality teams and community of practices generate innovative, high-quality solutions in agility. They are ideal contributors to digital transformation and fusion.

Recognising Blind Spots

Everyone can have blind spots. It is a natural and inevitable situation. Blind spots can be hazardous in certain circumstances. The owner of the blind spot cannot see his or her blind spot unless using specific tools or assistance from someone else.

Excellent technical leaders are astute and professional observers. They look for big pictures from multiple angles and can deep dive when needed hence can quickly identify blind spots and weaknesses.

These leaders also articulate situations with constructive feedback and help people to see their blind spots and understand their weaknesses and turn them to strengths.

Focus on Measures

Taking necessary measures are essential for digital

transformations. Excellent technical leaders focus on both qualitative and quantitative measures for team success. These excellent leaders manage across complex matrix structures in their organisations. They use KPIs (Key Performance Indicators). They use a team dashboard to see the trends and can qualify and quantify progress in visual formats for the team members and the business stakeholders.

These leaders also encourage other team members to create their dashboard and shared dashboard for the team. They turn the company to a data-driven organisation to measure the progress methodically.

One of the key measures is customer orientation and support mechanisms. These leaders ensure a customer-centric outlook is provided, focusing on continually improving client experience with measurable results.

Thought Leadership

Thought leadership is a critical need and demand in digital transformation environments, changing cultures, and transformating ecosystems. The primary thought leaders are excellent technical leaders in these environments.

These leaders can think digitally. They are digital thought leaders. In the past, we used to call them technology-minded leaders. We now use the term of digital thinkers and thought leaders. Some also call them digital opinion leaders.

Excellent technical leaders are drivers of ubiquitous digital transformations at a personal and organisational level. As almost every business has some digital transformation project to some extent, technical leaders leading these businesses must think digitally. They are thought leaders and at the forefront of digital transformations.

Tangible outcomes

Tangible outcomes are essential for the success of digital transformations. Digital transformation requires tangible outcomes iteratively rather than monolithic. For example, some tangible outcomes can be a virtualisation of platforms, creating containers, creating reusable shared resources, reviewed products, and agreed services.

Excellent technical transformation leaders pay special attention to providing tangible outcomes with the support of their team members. The transformation environment presents a constant and rapid change and any change matters in the transforming ecosystem.

These small and rapid changes lead to more significant tangible outcomes at later stages of the transformation; for example, the systems may need to be fully automated, loosely coupled, service-oriented, software-defined, self-learning, self-managing, and self-healing are a few to mention.

Background Makes Difference

The technology leaders who come from deep technical backgrounds and specialist level experience starting as a technical junior can be much different from a technology leader coming from a management background with limited technical knowledge, skills and experience.

While both types of leaders have value for the business, the dynamics can be very different from innovation, agility, collaboration, and technical excellence perspectives.

My observations reveal that selected technology leaders from extensive technical background coupled with excellent people skills can be more productive and effective in complex IT and digital transformation environments. These are exceptional hands-on leaders starting from the very bottom climbed to the highest level.

Ironically, not every technical person can be an excellent technical leader. Therefore, we need to explore the attributes that make a technical person an excellent technical or technology leader.

With all due respect to the leaders coming from the advanced management and leadership schools or other academic environments with years of experience, my observations revealed that most of these skilful people are true leaders, however, in general, they are not necessarily ideal candidates to be technical or technology leaders to make a real difference for substantial digital transformation initiatives. Of course, there are self-taught management professionals with utmost passion in technology who constitute the exceptions in some cases for leading complex digital transformation initiatives.

Chapter Summary and Key Points

Technical Eminence: Technical eminence requires not only expertise in technical areas but also all associated and related domains in a broader scope. Eminent leaders have strong industry skills, thought leadership, and multiple domain expertise. They are highly regarded and sought after for their views and contributions.

Communicators: Technical leaders are excellent communicators and can communicate at all levels with confidence and ease. They also encourage other people to communicate clearly and effectively to share their knowledge in the team or outside of the immediate teams.

Innovators: Technical leaders are excellent innovators and create an innovation culture and embed it to the organisations' ecosystem.

Mentoring and Coaching: Technical leaders are mentors and coach. Their mentoring and coaching capabilities help their team members to stretch themselves to bigger and better roles. They can coach team members as one on one and in a group.

Change Catalyst: Technical leaders are a catalyst for change; hence, they refresh the culture to more agile, collaborative and innovative ways.

Active Learners: They turn every possible interaction to a potential learning opportunity. They create learning opportunities for team members. They can also teach other people actively. By teaching, they even learn more and better.

Keeping Talent: Excellent technical leader understand the value and importance of talent for digital transformations. Keeping talent for technology leaders are essential. Talent is one of the critical enablers of core products and services of an organisation. Without talent, an organisation cannot be competitive.

Building High-Performance Teams: These leaders create proactive and engaged local technical teams and community of practices. These high-quality teams and community of practices generate innovative, high-quality solutions in agility.

Blind spots and Weakness: Technical leaders are astute and professional observers. They look for big pictures from multiple angles hence can quickly identify blind spots and weaknesses.

Taking all Measures: Excellent technical leaders focus on both qualitative and quantitative measures for team success. These excellent leaders manage across complex matrix structures in their organisations. They use KPIs (Key Performance Indicators). They use a team dashboard to see the trends and can qualify and quantify progress in visual formats for the team members and the business stakeholders.

Thought Leaders: Technical leaders can think digitally.

They are thought leaders and at the forefront of digital transformations.

Tangible Outcomes: Tangible outcomes are essential for the success of digital transformations. Digital transformation requires tangible outcomes iteratively rather than monolithic.

Background Difference: The technology leaders who come from deep technical background and experience starting as a technical junior can be much different from a technology leader coming from a management background with limited technical knowledge, skills and experience.

Chapter 8: Vital Technical Leadership Skills For Digital Transformation

Excellent technical leaders must possess a wide range of vital technical skills. There are many growing and emerging technologies that these leaders need to be conversant. These leaders focus on digital transformation enablers.

The key technology enablers of digital transformation are Cloud Computing, Mobile Technologies, IoT, Big Data, and Analytics. An integrated view of these technologies, associated processes and tools are critical. Besides, benchmarking of products and services are essential enablers of digital transformations.

In this section, we cover the key technologies and briefly introduce them by highlighting their importance for digital transformation goals. This is not an exhaustive list. The focus is only on the critical ones.

Let's touch on the critical technical skills that these leaders need to possess for leading successful digital transformation initiatives.

Cloud Computing

Cloud computing became mainstream in organisations. Adaptation of Cloud computing became very rapid. Cloud is used as a transformational tool. The cloud service model can expand or reduce computer resources based on service requirements. For example, Cloud can provide the maximum resources when we need a large amount of computing power or storage capacity for a specific task at a particular timeframe. Then we can release these resources after completing our specific mission. This elasticity and scalability provide value position for digital transformations.

'Pay per use' or 'pay as you go' is another essential characteristic that Cloud services model provides. The resources can be consumed based on the usage amount. Usage could be a short- or long-term basis. For example, consumers can pay based on computing power or storage amount they used. Related to 'pay per use', using 'on-demand' is another characteristic of the Cloud services model. Consumers can use when they demand the required services without upfront payment or dedicated investment for the IT resources in their organisation. The recent commercial trend for using virtual machines in publicly available Cloud services are based on three types of instances such as on-demand instance, reserved instance and spot instance. In on-demand instance, there is no long term commitment. Reserved instance is a relatively longer-term with a substantial discount compared to on-demand usage. The spot instance, the price is agreed based on bidding.

Cloud offers resiliency. This means that system failures such as servers or storage units can be automatically isolated with predefined instructions, and workloads are migrated to redundant virtual units without disrupting the service levels or consumer usage. Cloud's resilience attribute removes many of our supportability concerns in our solution requirements.

Based on consumer requirements, Cloud resources can be virtual or physical. This flexibility is created by multitenancy characteristic of the Cloud service model. For example, a Cloud service provider can host multiple user workloads in the same infrastructure without adversely affecting their privacy and security. If there are high-security requirements such as sensitive governmental services, isolation can be physical. We need to consider constraints and limitations which can affect the use of virtual services in multi-tenancy mode.

Flexible workload movement is another crucial attribute of Cloud service model. There may be times an organisation requires to run their workloads in a different time zone, and the workloads can easily be moved to a data centre in another country. This may be for several reasons such as reducing cost, providing a better service for a focus group in a different location or even regulatory requirements.

IoT (Internet of Things)

IoT (Internet of Things) is another vital technology that technology leaders need to understand. Substantial progress has been made in many disciplines owing to the use of IoT in creating new services and products. Some of these disciplines include environmental monitoring, manufacturing, infrastructure management, energy management, agriculture, healthcare, transportation, IT, electronics, material sciences and banking.

In the market, it is noticeable that IoT technologies are emerging and IoT solutions are growing exponentially. Some organisations estimate billions of devices in the next few years to connect to the global IoT ecosystem. The bottom line is that IoT is valuable for both business and economy, which is inevitable. From our current experience, we can construe that IoT will most likely have a substantial impact on our economy and the way we do business and commerce.

Consumers and service providers have an incredible interest and focus on this fantastic technology powered by the internet. The generation of new business for companies and new job roles that we cannot even name yet is imminent. Some believe that the IoT can be as important as the emergence of the internet itself. Some even point out that it can be the next big thing in our lives. These are, of course, speculations, combined with some media hype; however, time will tell as to whether the high expectations of IoT will be met. One key fact is that IoT is one of the primary enablers of the digital transformation; hence, it is an essential skill that these leaders need to possess.

Big Data, Analytics & Machine Learning

Big Data and Data Analytics are beneficial technology domains that technology leaders need to understand and use for creating insights and competitive advantage for their organisations.

Even though architecturally similar to traditional data, big data requires newer methods and tools to deal with data. The traditional methods and tools are not adequate to process big data. The process refers to capturing a substantial amount of data from multiple sources, storing analysing, searching, transferring, sharing, updating, visualising and governing huge volumes data such as petabytes or even exabytes.

Ironically, the main concern or aim of Big Data is not the amount of data but more advanced analytics techniques to produce value out of these large volumes of data. The advanced analytics in this context refers to approaches such as descriptive, predictive, prescriptive, and diagnostic analytics.

The descriptive analytics deals with situations such as what is happening right now based on incoming data. The predictive analytics refers to what might happen in the future. Prescriptive analytics deals with actions to be taken. Diagnostic analytics ask the question of why something happened. Each analytics type serves difference scenarios and use-cases.

Big Data Analytics is a comprehensive business-driven discipline. At a high level, it aims to make quick business decisions, reduce the cost for a product or service, and test new market to create new products and services. Big Data analytics are used in all industries; the most commonly used industries are health care, life sciences, manufacturing, government, and retail.

We need methods and tools to perform Big Data Analytics. There are established methods and many tools available on the market. Most of the methods are proprietary, but some are available via open-source programs. Some popular tools frequently mentioned in the Big Data Analytics publications are Aqua Data Studio, Azure HDinsight, IBM SPSS Modeler, Skytree, Talend, Splice Machine, Plotly, Lumify, Elasticsearch. In the appendix, there is a list of commercial service providers in these areas.

Besides, open-source has progressed well in this area and produced multiple powerful tools. Some commonly used open-source analytics tools are Apache Hadoop, Apache Spark, Apache Storm, Apache Cassandra, Apache SAMOA, Neo4j, MongoDB, and R programming environment. We cover the overview of these tools in the technology and tools section of this chapter.

Big Data analytics is a broad and growing area. We can better understand Big data analytics looking at its inherent characteristics. These characteristics can be summarised using nine 'C-terms' to remember easily. These terms are connection, conversion, cognition, configuration, content, customisation, cloud, cyber, and community. As these terms are self-explanatory, we don't go into details to explain each here.

Big Data analytics use various methods and techniques such as natural language processing, A/B testing, machine learning, data mining, association pattern mining, behavioural analytics, predictive analytics, descriptive analytics, prescriptive analytics, diagnostic analytics.

Machine Learning & Text Analytics

Machine learning refers to computer systems to learn and improve based on their learning from the analysis of large volumes of data sets without programming. It is part of the artificial intelligence domain in computer science. Due to its usefulness and impact, machine learning became a vital technology and tool for digital transformation.

Text analytics include computational linguistics, machine learning, and traditional statistical analysis. Text analytics focus on converting massive volumes of a machine or human-generated text into meaningful structures to create business insights and support decision-making.

There are various text analytics techniques. For example, IE (Information extraction) is one of the text analytics techniques which extract structured data from unstructured text. 'Text summarisation' is another technique which can automatically create a condensed summary of a document or selected groups of documents. This is especially useful for blogs, news, product documents, and scientific papers. NLP (Natural Language Processing) is another sophisticated text analytics technique interfaced as question and answers in natural language such as Siri in Apple products.

Cybersecurity

Security is a necessary skill for digital transformation. Cloud Computing, IoT and Big Data also mandate security at all levels. Broader security awareness and associated skills are essential for technology leaders leading digital transformation.

Cybersecurity is a vast security domain and touches every aspect of security management, such as identity management, authentication, authorisation, and many more areas. Cybersecurity is a critical factor in digital transformation solutions.

Related to advanced security, Blockchain, which is relatively new technology, is becoming critical for new security requirements which could be enablers for digital transformations.

Network

The network is another essential skills that technical leaders in digital transformation area must possess. Digital transformation solutions touch every aspect of networking such as wide area, local area, wireless and many more networking types. They proliferate as far as Cloud, IoT and Big Data are concerned.

Since the network and associated communication technologies are the fundamental enablers of digital transformations, understanding functions of network and network implications such as security, latency, bandwidth, are also important topics that technology leaders need to cover broadly and in-depth based on their involvement.

Mobility

Mobility is a critical technology stream in organisations hence the technology leaders need to understand and educate their teams for the effective use of mobility for innovations leading to business insights and collaboration across the organisation including the customers and partners.

The domain of Enterprise Mobile Management (EMM) includes essential components such as device management, application management, content management, email management, and unified endpoint management.

Mobility is associated with several architectural and business considerations such as network access, compliance, data management, workplace demographics, end-user accountability and BYOD (Bring Your Own Devices) concepts.

IT Service Management

IT service management covers an extensive array of technology, process, and tools. IT service management includes processes such as change management, problem management, incident management, service level management, capacity management, availability management, business continuity management, security management.

Also, system management processes such as monitoring, alerting, and event management can be covered under the umbrella term of IT Service Management. These processes are managed using many technological tools. More importantly, these tools need to be architected, integrated, designed and implemented coherently.

Understanding the dynamics of these tools within the context of digital transformation initiatives are vital for successful outcomes. One of the best representation of IT Service model is implemented using popular ITIL (Information Technology Infrastructure Library.

Technical Governance

Technical governance is an essential aspect of digital transformations. These transformations require particular governance model due to their nature. For example, a dynamic and flexible governance model may be required for digital transformation initiatives.

Technical leaders usually perform the role of technical governance head in sizeable digital transformation programs. They can have formal roles. For example, these leaders can run the architecture review boards or design authority forums established for complex digital transformation programs.

One of the common frameworks for technical governance in the industry is COBIT (Control Objectives for Information and related Technology). Use of the COBIT framework helps organisations gain optimal value from their IT investments by maintaining a balance between gaining benefits and optimising risk levels and resource use.

Architectural and Design Skills

Architecture is a critical aspect of digital transformation. If architecture goes wrong, everything else goes wrong. After architecture, the next important factor is the design in the transformation lifecycle. Digital transformation requires both architectural and design skills.

Excellent technical leaders hold these skills. They have strategic, architectural thinking, and design thinking skills. They need to articulate the current environment to the sponsoring executives, set future environment goals and show how to bridge the gap between these two environments.

At a high level, these leaders understand the overall scope, its requirements, and use cases of the solution. These leaders can assess risks, issues, dependencies in their day to day tasks.

Chapter Summary and Key Points

Cloud Computing: Cloud Computing is essential for digital transformation; hence, it is a critical skill. Adaptation of Cloud computing became very rapid. Cloud is used as a transformational tool. The cloud service model can expand or reduce computer resources based on service requirements.

Internet of Things: IoT (Internet of Things) is a vital technology; hence, technology leaders need to understand it well. Substantial progress has been made in many disciplines owing to the use of IoT in creating new services and products. In the market, it is noticeable that IoT technologies are emerging and IoT solutions are growing exponentially.

Big Data: Even though architecturally similar to traditional data, big data requires newer methods and tools to deal with data. The traditional methods and tools are not adequate to process big data. The process refers to capturing a substantial amount of data from multiple sources, storing analysing, searching, transferring, sharing, updating, visualising and governing huge volumes data such as petabytes or even exabytes.

Big Data Analytics: Big Data Analytics is a comprehensive business-driven discipline. At a high level, it aims to make quick business decisions, reduce the cost for a product or service, and test new market to create new products and services. Big Data analytics are used in all industries; the most commonly used industries are health care, life sciences, manufacturing, government, and retail.

Machine Learning: Machine learning refers to computer systems to learn and improve based on their learning from the analysis of large volumes of data sets without programming. It is part of the artificial intelligence domain in computer science. Due to its usefulness and impact, machine learning became a vital technology and tool for digital transformation.

Text Analytics: Text analytics include computational linguistics, machine learning, and traditional statistical analysis. Text analytics focus on converting massive volumes of a machine or human-generated text into meaningful structures to create business insights and support decision-making.

Cybersecurity: Broader cybersecurity awareness and associated skills are essential for technology leaders leading digital transformation. Cybersecurity is a vast security domain and touches every aspect of security management, such as identity management, authentication, authorisation, and many more areas.

Network: understanding functions of network and network implications such as security, latency, bandwidth, are also important topics that technology leaders need to cover broadly and in-depth based on their involvement.

Mobility: Mobility is a critical technology stream in organisations hence the technology leaders need to understand and educate their teams for the effective use of mobility for innovations leading to business insights and collaboration across the organisation including the customers and partners.

IT Service Management: IT service management covers an extensive array of technology, process, and tools. IT service management includes processes such as change management, problem management, incident management, service level management, capacity management, availability management, business continuity management, security management.

Technical Governance: Technical governance is an essential aspect of digital transformations. Technical leaders usually perform the role of technical governance head in sizeable digital transformation programs. They can also run the architecture review board or design authority forums.

Architectural and Design Skills: Technical leaders need to articulate the current environment to the sponsoring executives, set future environment goals and show how to bridge the gap between these two environments. At a high level, they understand the overall scope, requirements, and use cases. They can assess risks, issues, dependencies in their day to day tasks.

Chapter 9: Conclusions

We covered several crucial attributes of technical and technology leaders. This book highlighted their excellence. We know that technical leaders strive for excellence rather than perfection. Excellence refers to having or demonstrating outstanding quality for the leaders for making a noticeable impact on other people, especially on the followers. These leaders must demonstrate tolerance to uncertainty and ambiguity. Taking risk is one of the necessities and most fundamental characteristics of leaders for success.

Dealing with people and leading others require robust emotional intelligence. Emotional intelligence makes the leaders more self-aware with their fluctuating moods, changing emotions, and drives. Interacting with people and feeling comfortable with many personalities is a core requirement of social intelligence. Socially intelligent leaders are outgoing yet courteous, tactful and diplomatic in their approach. Mindful leaders can cope with massive stress caused by hectic workplaces, volatile business situations, and ever-changing technologies effectively.

Taking personal responsibility and being accountable for the situations technical leaders can leave better impressions on their followers. This positive disposition creates a trust for our integrity. Excellent leaders are action-oriented. They prioritise their tasks and act immediately based on their priorities. They don't like delaying necessary actions. They dislike procrastination.

Leadership vision needs to display the values, beliefs, and culture of the organisation. Leaders' vision brings team members together; hence, they work for the same goals. Resourceful technical leaders are capable of understanding the current situation, having a vision for the future state, articulating the needs to all stakeholders, and developing a pathway to reach the target state effectively using the talented team members who are following them.

Priority management is focusing on essential tasks which make a real difference for desired outcomes. Focusing on things that matter, avoiding distractions, removing roadblocks, creating enablers are fundamental characteristics of leaders to set the prioritisation for the digital transformation. These leaders employ various techniques to reach consensus. They can clarify rules of engagement for all parties, operating models in the organisation or departments, and underlying processes and procedures.

Effective communication requires unbiased listening, understanding others point of views and conveying the message to the point in the right context. Clarity is one of the critical enablers of effective communication. Using the right words in the right context, refraining from jargons and ambiguous words are essential to effective communication. These leaders learn new situations quickly in the right context. They adjust themselves to the situations based on their capability to learn quickly, respond intelligently, and follow up efficiently.

Excellent technical leaders are known as quiet achievers. They don't highlight their achievement and success overtly. Most of the time, they leave it to others to recognise and appreciate them rather than self-promoting their cases. They stand up when necessary. Paying attention to people's current moods, body language, tone of voice and other clues from their conversations, excellent leaders can steer conversations in healthier and productive ways.

Influence requires several leadership characteristics and capabilities. One of the primary characteristics is building trust with people. Trust built with integrity is believed to open all communication channels in the workplace. Besides, these leaders are principle oriented. We accept principles as determining truth for our conversations, actions and interactions. It is useless to argue against principles because they are based on truth.

Technical leaders create a meaningful sense of urgency to change people and situations to better conditions. They are self-aware and confident. Self-aware leaders naturally have self-confidence. Self-confident leaders take more calculated risks to create better opportunities. Self-aware and self-confident leaders connect better with other people. Their communication styles are noticeably bright and articulate. They are optimistic people, and they focus on good things to happen.

Physical, mental and emotional energy is essential for leaders to shine. They know how to energise themselves at the right dose and right times. Their noticeable energy also inspires other people to gain energy to achieve their goals. These leaders recognise the distractions, especially hidden ones, and don't waste their energy on them. Focusing on priorities naturally lowers the impact of distractions.

Excellent leaders build trust based on integrity. These fundamental human traits, trust and integrity, apply to all walks of life and crucial for leadership in all domains. These leaders are transparent and open about their thoughts, views, ideas, vision, goals, and objectives. They even encourage opposing views shared with respect.

Modest leaders admit their mistakes with humility without self-degrade. They embrace new ideas and don't resist their views as being superior to others. They refrain from dominating the conversations and discussion sessions. They are also charismatic to their followers. In general, charismatic leaders are effective communicators; people like listening to them and follow them with passion. Followers hardly question the credibility of charismatic leaders as people are mesmerised by their gentle attitudes, engaging conversations and other pleasant characteristics.

We also understand that these excellent technical leaders naturally have a growth mindset rather than a fixed mindset. Leaders with a growth mindset are more resilient in life, more motivated, can deal with situations more effectively, develop better relationships, communicate more clearly, hence achieve better results.

After excellence, as the second pillar of our framework, we introduced innovation as a critical factor of digital transformations. Novelty is a critical ingredient of innovation. Innovative processes focus on novelty, improvement, and ongoing progress. Innovative thinking generates novel ideas, focus on improving ideas, and strive for making iterative progress.

Innovation feeds the culture and is a critical aspect of an ecosystem in organisations. Cultures embracing innovation can naturally renew themselves for surviving and thriving. They extend to the next generations with constant progress. People collaborate better in innovative cultures. They see themselves with the changing conditions in new positions. Technical leaders in these cultures help to remove roadblocks for innovation. It is critical to recognise innovation blockers and show stoppers. The roadblocks to innovation can be from various angles. One of the main showstoppers is keeping the status quo.

Harnessing and driving creative thinking result in innovation. For excellent leaders, innovation turns to habit or more accurately a lifestyle. The horizontal type of thinking is beneficial for creating innovations. There are different techniques that we can use for horizontal thinking. Some commonly used techniques are randomisations, distortions, reversals, exaggerations, metaphors, analogies, dreaming, theme mining, questioning the norms, and creating contradictions. Technical leaders demonstrate a growth mindset to ignite innovation. Growth mindset leading towards innovation is a build-in characteristic in these leaders' personalities.

As our third pillar in our framework, we introduced the importance of simplicity at various levels. Ironically, to create simplicity, we need to deal with a lot of complexity, complications and sophisticated matters. Obtaining the required knowledge, acquiring advanced skills, and gaining substantial experience are not easy and not indeed simple activities. Paradoxically, we need to deal with complexity to create simplicity.

User-centric excellent leaders ask the question of how they can create products and services simple, intuitive, and human-centric. The consumer-oriented simplicity is a requirement for leading innovative teams. Simplifying processes are critical. Consumers keep complaining that technology creates complexity and make it difficult to understand concepts and objects in natural human language.

The services model requires substantial amounts of simplification for users to take benefits of using technologies. Service simplification is essential for digital transformation and adds substantial value to the business from every angle.

Applying design thinking, combined with adopting agile methods for design, is one of the simplification approaches. The digital trends, mobile culture and agile approaches made substantial changes in addressing the cumbersome specifications, especially concerning the users or consumers. The deep-down technical details for user specifications were found unnecessary. Agile methods proposed simplifications of cumbersome specifications in user stories format.

The simplification process for communication is

essential and enables to facilitate understanding of issues, risks and dependencies effectively. The right context in simplifying the language is also required. It is essential to balance qualitative and quantitative aspects while conveying a message to the audience. Complex and complicated governance processes and procedures can be a hurdle for digital transformation. They can cause delays, confusions, rework and low performance for the transformation initiatives. Therefore, it is critical to simplify governance framework, process and procedures for digital transformation.

Data and analytics simplicity are also critical for digital transformations. The simplicity for data can be achieved through the use of streamlined data sources, effective data processing, accurate data analysis, introducing intelligence, effective management strategies, and powerful tools. In other words, when correctly and purposefully analysed, more data can add better intelligence for digital transformations.

As the fourth pillar for our framework, we touched on agility from various angles. We know that technology leaders in this digital era must be agile to be influential, competitive and productive in their fields. It is almost impossible to succeed with old methods as many organisations focus on adapting to agility and on the way of maturing their delivery at a rapid pace. Besides, we know that consumers demand services very rapidly.

We discussed generations of gaps for adopting agile in large organisations. Agile is a particular interest to the new generations as they grow with agility in all walks of life. However, the older generation still has a sentimental attachment to waterfall methods.

Technical leaders develop mental models on how technology users interact with their solution in each iteration. With their action-oriented approach, they use the backlogs quickly and in priority orders. They engage in pragmatic architecture to maintain agility. Architecture involves things that are hard to change later. However, this doesn't mean we cannot apply agile to architecture. There is a massive trend to use Agile methods for developing architectural solutions.

There are many evolving Agile methods to support different kinds of development processes. Developers embrace Agile methods. They can see the results much more quickly. Use of evolving methods such as DevOps is also prime considerations for enabling digital transformations. Agile methods have a particular focus on automation. Automation enables simplifying and speeding up processes.

Agile approaches require moving from silos to a flatter structure to resolve the issues of isolated and hierarchical structures in large organisations. Priority is set by using various considerations. One of the critical aspects is the creation of a minimum viable product using the Agile method. A Sprint is the shortest time bombed duration to create the minimum viable product.

Agile methods mandate change. Change management is a vital aspect of Agile methods. Embracing change is critical to be successful in agile delivery. Adapting to constant change is very important for agility. Agile methods enable the principles of the fail fast, fail early, fail cheaply. Of course, failure is not for the sake for failure, no one enjoys failure, but it is beneficial to fail earlier than later to keep the cost of failure low and be successful in the long run from the lessons learnt from small failures.

Agile is a cost-focused and revenue-generating approach. Technical leaders can manage costs better and generate more revenue by adopting agile approaches in high impact tasks and solution development activities in their organisations. Through incremental progress, prioritised backlog management, speedy iterative delivery through

Sprints, the cost of failure for big chunks of work items can be prevented. Also, the costs can be turned into revenues.

As the fifth pillar in our excellence framework, we covered collaboration and fusion. We can define collaboration as a team of people working together for mutual goals. The team and mutual goals are essential entities of this simple framework. We should also focus on the work aspect of the collaboration rather than entertainment or hobbies. Fusion principles aim to bring individuals from various backgrounds, small groups with different purposes, various teams with differing capabilities, communities of practices with different missions under a single umbrella for serving a mission.

Once technical leaders initiate collaborative activities and invite their collaborators, then the process is maintained with necessary communication and engagement rules. Effective communication is a critical enabler of collaboration.magic of collaboration starts with these repetitions. Successful repetitions make ripple effects for more success. In a relatively short time frame, these teams create a collaborative culture aligned with the organisation's ecosystem and strategic goals.

Technical leaders influence their collaborators with their responsibility, accountability and demonstrated credibility. They earn the trust of their collaborators. Strategic technical leaders pay special attention to remain credible in their fields. These leaders pay special attention to diversity and inclusiveness to maintain a collaborative fusion. Diversity is an enhancer of collaboration. More importantly, with diversity, also innovation pops up again. Diverse ideas ignite innovation.

Exploring the crucial characteristics of these excellent technical leaders presented concisely in this book can provide valuable insights for their engagements for digital transformational leadership initiatives. Reviewing the capabilities of these leaders by using a pragmatic five-pillar framework can add clarity to understand their leadership and contributions to the demands of digital transformation initiatives. These critical technical leadership skills, capabilities, and attributes can be instrumental for aspiring technical leaders to understand and apply them for leading future digital transformation engagements.